All-Terrain Pushchair Walks

Argyll and Lochaber

Zoë Sayer and Elizabeth Cottier

Published by Sigma Leisure – an imprint of
Sigma Press, Stobart House, Pontyclerc, Penybanc Road
Ammanford, Carmarthenshire SA18 3HP

British Library Cataloguing in Publication Data

A CIP record for this book is available from the British Library

ISBN: 978-1-85058-860-3

Typesetting and Design by: Sigma Press, Ammanford, Wales

Cover Photograph: Cruachan Dam, Taynuilt by Oban © Zoë Sayer

Maps: Zoë Sayer

Photographs: Zoë Sayer, Keith Jackson, Elizabeth Cottier and Finlo Cottier

Printed by: Cromwell Press Group, Trowbrige, Wiltshire

Disclaimer: The information in this book is given in good faith and is believed to be correct at the time of publication. Care should always be taken when walking in hill country. Where appropriate, attention has been drawn to matters of safety. The author and publisher cannot take responsibility for any accidents or injury incurred whilst following these walks. Only you can judge your own fitness, competence and experience. Do not rely solely on sketch maps for navigation: we strongly recommend the use of appropriate Ordnance Survey (or equivalent) maps.

Preface

The outstanding scenery and feeling of wilderness throughout Argyll and Lochaber makes this a fantastic location in which to introduce your children to walking and the outdoors. It is great to get them out in the fresh air from as early an age as possible so that they can experience the delights of the world around them and give them a healthy outlook for life! This area has so much to offer from spectacular beaches, ideal for a picnic, riverside walks and, if you're lucky, the chance to glimpse a roe deer, white tailed eagle or even a minke whale! There are also castles, railways and lighthouse towers, as well as natural features such as fields and hedgerows, spectacular rocks, woodland filled with wild bluebells and panoramic views out to the islands of the Inner Hebrides. Every experience you give your child increases their knowledge and the area has so much to offer, making it the perfect place to introduce your children to the delights of the outdoors.

All-terrain pushchairs have finally made the great outdoors accessible to parents and the obstacles found in the countryside far easier to negotiate. There is no longer any reason why having a baby should deter us from getting out and about in the countryside. Argyll and Lochaber is a great area in which to use these pushchairs having an extensive network of forestry and cycle tracks. However, it is often difficult to plan a walk from a map as details of stiles and narrow kissing gates are not available and narrow rocky pathways are not always shown. This book contains thirty tried and tested pushchair walks in Argyll and Lochaber, which will allow you to go for a walk and explore the delights of the region with full knowledge of the route ahead.

The walks were selected to provide you with a wide variety of walks from simple riverside and coastal rambles to more ambitious hill climbs, where the view from the top more than makes up for the breathlessness on the way up (!), so there is something for everyone. Walk selection is straight forward with our 'at a glance' symbol key, which provides information on refreshments, changing facilities, etc. Each walk also has background information around the route and a selection of 'in the area' activities for other ways to amuse the whole family, particularly if it's raining!

We have really enjoyed putting this book together and hope that you and your children enjoy the walks as much as we did.

Zoë Sayer and Liz Cottier

Acknowledgements

Special thanks to Rhodri, Rhiannon and Ruari for being the test subjects for this book! Thanks also to Keef and Finlo and various other friends who acted as guinea pigs on many of these walks.

Contents

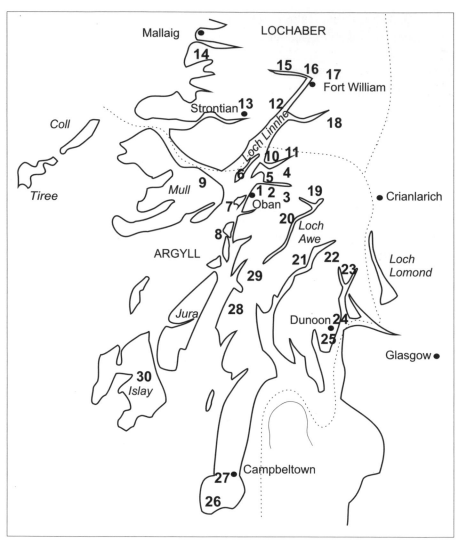

Location of Walks

Introduction

This book contains thirty walks in Argyll and Lochaber suitable for an all-terrain pushchair. There are both circular and 'there-and-back' routes, and many can be shortened or have worthwhile detours. Walks range from 1 to 6 miles in length and cover a wide range of difficulty, which we hope will cater for all types of walkers. The walks encompass both the mainland and the Argyll islands, so, hopefully, you will find a suitable walk nearby, wherever you are. The walks are not exhaustive and are intended as an introduction to the area. We've tried to include walks that are close to trunk roads and major towns and, in the case of the islands, easily accessed from the main ferry terminals.

Routes and Grades

We have purposefully made the layout of this book as easy to follow as possible. Each walk is accompanied by a simple route map showing the start point and numbers referring to details in the text, as well as obvious features. The maps are intended to be used in conjunction with the relevant Ordnance Survey Explorer map, and the information on them is by no means comprehensive. Details of the relevant map and the starting grid reference are given in the walk summary.

Each walk contains an 'at-a-glance' key which tells you all about the walk – distance, difficulty, any stiles, facilities such as toilets or ice cream vans and any hidden costs, so there shouldn't be any nasty surprises when you set off. You can also see whether the walk requires two people to overcome obstacles or if it can be accomplished solo.

The walks have a basic summary, detailing points of interest and useful information around the route. We have also included an 'in the area' section, suggesting nearby alternative activities for you and your family.

You should always allow more time than that recommended. Times given are approximate and based on a speed of two miles an hour. However, not everyone walks at the same speed and the times given do not make allowances for picnics, tantrum breaks or walking toddlers.

Please note: circular routes are written in the direction that requires the least effort and are not always reversible! If you are thinking of reversing a walk, read the description carefully to check if it is possible.

Fitness

It is assumed that walkers will have a basic level of fitness. Those who consider themselves unfit should only attempt the easiest level of walk and, if necessary, take advice from their doctor. The hardest level of walk should only be attempted by those experienced in both mountain walking and all-terrain pushchair technique.

All-Terrain Pushchairs – advice for first-time buyers

There are now many makes of all-terrain pushchairs (ATP) on the market, as well as trendy 3-wheeler strollers most of which are designed for urban use. To help ease this confusion and choose a genuine ATP, here are some of the factors you need to consider if you want to take your pushchair off-road.

Ensure your child is old enough for the ATP. Many makes have a reclining position suitable for use from birth, but bear in mind that very young babies should not be bumped around. Seek the manufacturer's advice and choose your walks carefully. Small babies (less than four months) should only be taken on the easiest level of walks and never over rough ground. If you don't like the look of the terrain, turn back!

Make sure the ATP has pneumatic tyres and good suspension to provide cushioning. Lightweight prams are better!

Choose a long wheel-base, which makes leverage over obstacles easier than a short wheel-base. The front wheel should be fixed, or, at the very least, lockable. Rear wheels should be quick release.

Check the pushchair folds easily and that it fits in the boot of your car!

Shop around as it is always worth looking in the shops first and then checking the internet for the same pram at a better price – either new or used.

Accessories

A rain cover is essential, especially when out walking in the hills as the weather can change very quickly. Good quality footmuffs are easily available, if not already included in the price; fleece-lining and/or windproofing provides extra comfort.

Sunshades supplement the hood, which generally doesn't extend enough for walking uphill into full sun. Mesh shades are easier to walk with than parasols and also provide protection against midges.

A puncture repair kit and pump are strongly advisable for those emergency situations. You can also fill the tyres with a 'goo' designed as an emergency fix for bicycle tyres and which prevents serious deflation, or buy thorn-proof inner tubes.

We've found a pram leash is essential, especially on walks with steep drops or descents. This is a strap, climbing sling or piece of rope tied to the pram handle and fastened to your wrist. This provides extra security should you accidentally let go of the pushchair, and is more secure than a handbrake.

What to take

For the baby:
Pram – rain cover, sun cover, footmuff and puncture repair kit.
Milk – if you are not breastfeeding, formula milk is easily carried in ready made cartons or powder sachets, then just add to water in bottles when you need it. If your baby likes warm milk, either carry warm water in a flask or make up extra hot milk and wrap in foil or a muslin.
Nappies, wipes and nappy bag.
Picnic – sandwiches are easy if your baby eats on his/her own, otherwise take fruit pots, yogurt or anything easy to open. Don't forget a spoon and take all rubbish home with you.
Snacks – to cheer up a bored or peckish baby until you find a picnic spot. We have found that raisins or baby crisps keep them occupied for the longest!
Water/juice.
Spare clothes – layers are best as they can easily be put on or taken off as conditions change. Don't forget that though you may be hot walking uphill, your baby is sitting still in the pushchair. Keep checking he/she is not too cold. An all in one fleece is a good buy. Look for one with fold-over ends to keep hands and feet warm – easier than gloves.
Hat – sunhat or woolly hat depending on the weather conditions.
Shoes or wellies – depending on the weather.

For you:
Shoes – check the guide at the start of the walk for appropriate footwear.
Waterproof – keep in the pram ready for emergencies.
Food and drink – it's very easy to forget your own in the rush to pack your baby's feast!

Mobile phone – be aware that coverage for some mobile phone networks cannot always be relied on in some remote areas.
Small first aid kit.
This guidebook and the relevant **Ordnance Survey map** for the walk.

The Scottish Outdoor Access Code

Scotland has a different approach to access compared to England and Wales. There are no rights of way as such, instead everyone has a statutory right of access and this applies to all land and inland waters. However, land must be accessed responsibly and with respect for land owners and other land users.

This right of access excludes houses and adjacent garden/land, land around and used by schools, building sites, commercial buildings and adjacent land, mature grassland which may be damaged by access and land planted with crops. Hunting, shooting, fishing and motor vehicles are not permitted, and dogs MUST be kept under control.

In addition, respect people's privacy and peace of mind. Help land managers and others to work safely and effectively – do not hinder land management operations and follow advice from land managers.

Respect requests for reasonable limitations on when and where you can go (e.g. forestry operations or stalking).

Care for your environment.

Do not disturb wildlife, leave the environment as you find it, follow a path or track if there is one and leave gates as you find them.

Keep your dog under proper control – do not take it through fields of calves and lambs, and clean up its waste – apart from being unpleasant, dog faeces contains a parasite that can make children blind.

For further information on the Scottish Outdoor Access Code, visit www.outdooraccess-scotland.com

Why walk?

Walking makes you feel good.
Walking reduces stress.
Walking helps you see more of your surroundings.
Walking helps you return to your pre-pregnancy figure.
Walking helps your baby learn about his/her surroundings and nature
.

Argyll and Lochaber

Argyll and Lochaber is an area of outstanding natural beauty, breathtaking seascapes, historic castles, white sandy beaches and even the odd glimpse of a minke whale, roe deer or white tailed eagle if you're lucky! It has a varied terrain, from dense lush woodland forests smothered in bluebells in spring, hidden inland lochans and wild open moorland to the often exhilarating rugged coastlines lined with the famous Machair (or grassland) and expansive empty beaches. From gentle riverside strolls, to isolated mountain glens and even a beach or two, we hope we have included something for everyone.

Given the varied terrain, it is an excellent area for pushchair walks due to the extensive network of forestry commission and national cycle tracks which span the entire region. The area is extremely popular with hill walkers and cyclists, therefore these tracks are generally well maintained.

We've chosen a selection of walks to show you the amazing variety of scenery on offer in the area, as well as different degrees of difficulty! The area is also rich in legend, history and geology, which we've tried to cover to some extent in the walk descriptions. The walks range from gentle strolls through glens famous for their archaeological heritage to riverside rambles in castle grounds to a spectacular but strenuous climb to the famous Cruachan Reservoir, high on the mountainside of Ben Cruachan.

The walks are across farmland, moorland, along coastal paths and through forestry on a combination of forest tracks and access paths. In Scotland, everyone has the right to access land for recreational purposes, although please be aware that although accessible at the time of writing, some routes may be closed for logging or deer stalking at certain times of the year.

Routes along beaches and some coastal sections can be affected by the tides. If a walk is tide-dependent we have mentioned this in the introduction and an alternative, there-and-back route is described if possible. Please note that you could get stranded by particularly high tides and take steps to avoid this. Tide tables are available in most outdoor shops and tourist information centres. Many national newspapers publish tide times and heights (usually on the weather page) or they can be checked on www.bbc.co.uk/weather/coast/tides/.

When crossing farmland, always pay due consideration to livestock. Keep dogs on a lead, older children under control and never disturb any animal that you come across. In addition, herds of cows can be problematic and have (fortunately rarely) been known to kill humans by stampeding. We have known cows to be particularly interested in the pushchair! If you are in any doubt as to your safety leave the field by the nearest possible exit and abandon the walk.

Scotland is famous for its scenery but also its midges! Rife from early May until October, though harmless, these wee beasties can be very annoying. The prevailing breezes often keep these at bay but on still days you will need to take some form of insect repellent. The pushchair can be protected with a fine mesh cover. Adults and older children should be covered up as much as possible, with any exposed skin protected with one of the various repellents on the market. Locals use 'Skin so Soft' by a well known cosmetics company, which you can find on sale in many of the local shops.

Another countryside menace is the tick, which is common in sheep and deer country. Ticks in Scotland carry Lyme's Disease, which can be particularly nasty. Again, cover up as much as possible and do a 'tick check' on you and your family after walking through grassland – look for small black dots, which may look like freckles and remove as soon as possible, preferably within 24 hours. Tick removal kits can be bought or you can remove them by covering the tick with Vaseline or massaging with a moist finger until the tick lets go. If bitten, keep an eye on the bite and if a 'bull's eye' rash or flu-like symptoms appear, go to your doctor.

Always remember the weather can change very rapidly and there can be few landmarks if the fog descends! Make sure you are equipped for all conditions and if in doubt turn back and return the way you came.

Transport

Finally, a few useful facts to help you on your way. The main tourist destinations are well connected by public transport, including ferries, buses and trains. Information and timetables are available at tourist information centres or they can be checked on www.visitscottishheartlands.com (Argyll) and www.visithighlands.com (Lochaber), www.calmac.co.uk (ferry), www.westcoastmotors.co.uk or www.citylink.co.uk (bus) and www.scotrail.co.uk (rail).

Key to Symbols

☺	Easy walk	🚧	Stile/obstacle
☺	Moderate walk	£	Parking/entry/ferry fee
☺	Strenuous walk	**WC**	Toilets
↻	Circular route	☕	Tea shop
↔	There-and-back	🍺	Pub
👟	Trainers suitable	🪑	Picnic area
👢	Wellies needed	🦆	Ducks
🥾	Walking boots essential	🍦	Ice cream van/shop
🧍	Achievable solo	🚂	Train/railway
🧍🧍	Two people needed	🛝	Playground
🛒	Suitable for double ATPs	🛷	Suitable for buggy boards

Walk 1: Polvinster Duck Pond and McCaig's Tower, Oban

Polvinster Duck Pond is just a stone's throw from the centre of Oban and is en route to one of the most famous landmarks in Oban: McCaig's Tower. The views are amazing from the tower, out over Oban's Distillery and across to the distant hills of Mull and the Morvern Peninsula.

This walk starts at Oban Railway Station and takes you away from the bustle of the town centre, out towards the sports' fields and golf course, past a tranquil lochan, complete with ducks, and on to McCaig's Tower (or 'Folly') with its imposing 'Roman Coliseum' style façade. The walk then takes you back down into the town via the main playpark and leisure centre. The path is on the whole well maintained and there are a few short steep inclines to be negotiated.

Distance:	1.9 miles (3 km)
Allow:	1 hour 30 mins
Map:	Ordnance Survey 1:25 000 OL 376
Grid reference:	298858

Getting there: Oban Railway Station is located in the centre of Oban, just off the A85 and next to the clock tower. It is right by the main bus terminal and opposite the Caledonian Hotel.

From the railway station, turn right and walk past a coffee shop on your right to the junction at Argyll Square. Cross the road and follow main road (A816) past the Royal Hotel and the Clydesdale Bank, signposted for Lochgilphead (Combie Street). Continue along this road, ignoring turnings on your left, until you reach the Kilmore and Kilbride Parish Church with its large spire.

1. At the church, turn left into Glencruitten Road and follow the road for approximately 0.5 km, until you reach Polvinster Road on your left.

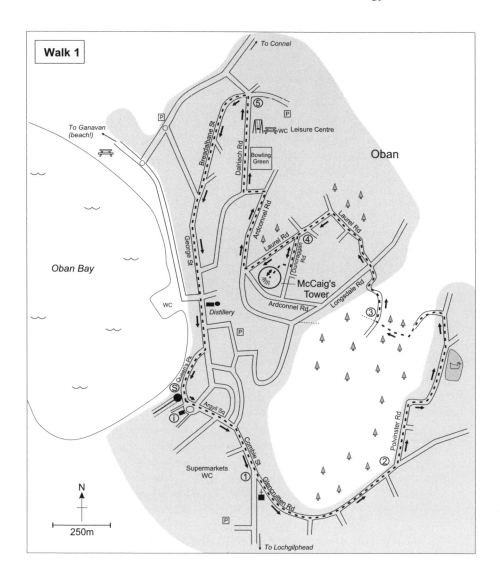

2. Turn on to Polvinster Road and ascend the short steep hill until
   the road plateaus out. Ignore a cul-de-sac on your right, bear right
   at the next junction and head uphill until you reach the tranquil
   lochan (small lake) on your right hand side. Continue along the
   road past several houses until you reach a fork in the road.

Ducks are always present and if you're lucky you may also catch a glimpse of a heron fishing in the shallow waters at the edge of the lochan.

Take the left hand fork to continue straight ahead and turn left at the next fork, up a road marked 'Private Road'. Ascend a short steep hill until you reach the end of the tarmac road. Pass through the wooden gate straight ahead of you and walk along the grassy path until you pass through a second gate to reach another metalled single track road.

3. Turn right onto the road and follow it down-hill until you reach a cross-roads. Take the road straight ahead (Laurel Road) and follow this road past a left turn to Laurel Crescent and bear left at the next junction, until you reach McCaig's Tower. Turn left down Duncraggen Road and walk past the car park on your right until you reach metal fencing on your right. Turn right here and through the large kissing gate to go up the easy access path to the tower itself.

McCaig's Tower was built almost one hundred years ago at a cost of £5,000 (quite a considerable sum in those days!) as a means of keeping local stonemasons in work during the winter months. Based on the Coliseum in Rome, it was unfortunately never finished, as the death of the wealthy benefactor John Stuart McCaig meant that the money ran out and the tower never did get its roof!

4. To head back into the town centre via the play park, return to the car park, turn left and follow Laurel Road as it descends steeply to a junction with Ardconnel Road.
   Turn right and follow Ardconnel Road as it descends into the town. Follow the road round a sharp left hand bend and then turn right onto Dalriach Road. Pass the bowling green on your right hand side and the play park is another 100 metres ahead on the right.

Toilets, café and indoor activities, including a soft play centre, are all found in the leisure centre next to the playpark.

5. To head back to the Railway Station, continue along Dalriach Road, and at the next junction turn left onto Breadalbane Street. Continue until the end of the road and turn left again onto the main road (George Street), which runs through the centre of Oban. Pass the

Having fun in McCaig's Tower, Oban

cinema and distillery on your left hand side, walk along the front with the sea on your right and turn right by the traffic lights into Queen's Park to return to the Railway Station.

Look out for the swans, seals and dolphins that are regular visitors to the bay and watch out for the rowdy seagulls that are only too happy to help themselves to your lunch if left unguarded!

In the area
Atlantis Leisure Centre, Oban is the town's main sports and leisure centre. Large swimming pool with flume, toddler pool, soft play, climbing wall, gym, outdoor play park and café. Open all year, 7 days a week. www.atlantisleisure.co.uk Tel: 01631 566800

Walk 2:
Glencruitten House Woods, Oban

Glencruitten House dates from 1897 and stands on a wooded hillside to the south of Oban, a short drive from the town centre. From its vantage point on the hillside there are spectacular views out towards Oban Bay and the islands of Kerrera and Mull. The present owners have upgraded the woodland footpaths and opened them to the public with waymarked routes and information boards.

This route takes you around the woods to a secret garden, view points, lakes and a tree cathedral. The route is steep in places but the two steepest sections are avoidable by following the alternative directions.

Distance:	2.5 miles (4 km)
Allow:	1 hour 30 mins
Map:	Ordnance Survey 1:25 000 OL376
Grid reference:	881296

Getting there: From Oban, turn off the A830 and head up Glencruitten road by the parish church with a tall spire. Pass the houses and go under the railway bridge. Turn into the woods by the lodge at the top of the hill. Park in the signposted car park.

From the car park, head along the woodland path by the information board with the house behind you and a lake on your right (look out for the chickens!). At the next junction turn right and go around the gate (to the left is easiest) and continue to the triangular junction.

1. Go straight ahead here and head uphill to the right of a green marker post. Follow the broad stony track until you reach a red marker. Turn left by the red marker and go uphill along a grassy path.

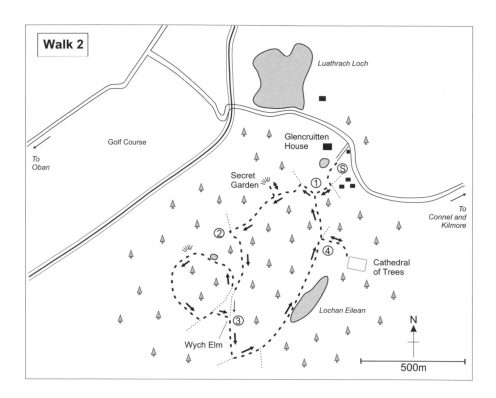

To visit the secret garden and first viewpoint, when you reach the fork turn right to head up the steep, stony path with a sign saying 'No Horses'. This takes you, via three awkward stony steps, to a bench with a spectacular view over Oban Bay. **To avoid the steep section, just continue straight ahead until you reach the forest track at 2.**

Ahead you can see the town of Oban laid out around the bay. Across the water is the island of Kerrera with Hutchison's Monument at its northern-most end. Beyond in the distance is Mull, and you may see the ferries heading across the water, past the white lighthouse at the southern end of Lismore.

Head back down the steep hill to return to the grassy path and turn right to rejoin the main route. Walk downhill, stony in places, until you reach a junction by a red marker post.

2. Turn left to join a broad forest track. Follow the track downhill to the next junction, where you turn right along a small path linking to a parallel track on your right. **To avoid this steep section, continue straight ahead along the main track until the Wych Elm at 3.**

   Turn right along the track and head steeply uphill and round to the left through conifers. Continue past a pond and at the top of the hill there is a second viewpoint with a large bench for admiring the view.

This takes in the western end of Oban with Glenshellach and the moorland beyond, the southern end of Kerrera and Mull in the distance.

Carry on past the bench and downhill to a T-junction. Turn left here and look out for a small, unmarked woodland path on your right. Turn right down the path and head steeply downhill to a T-junction to rejoin the forest track you left earlier.

The Cathedral of Trees

3. Turn right by a blue post onto the track.

   The tree at this junction is a Wych Elm. It's a lovely big tree and while it may not seem particularly spectacular, this tree is one of the rare survivors of Dutch Elm disease which ravaged the British Elm population during the 1970s and 1980s. Once common, Elms are now increasingly rare and it's lovely to see a surviving specimen.

   Continue following the main track as it heads round to the left, ignoring two turnings on the right. Carry on past a lake on your right, Lochan Eilean.

4. At the next triangular junction, turn sharp right to see the Tree Cathedral. Follow the grassy path around to the right until you reach a gate on the left.

   Through the arch is the Cathedral of Trees, which has yew trees planted in the form of a church with pillars, choir stalls, side chapels and an aisle. This was the burial ground for the family of Alexander McKay, a businessman who, in the early 1900s, implemented the planting of the woodlands you have just walked through.

   Return to the main track and turn right to return to the large triangular junction you passed at the start of the walk. Turn right and go back round the gate, and then left down the gravel path to return to the car park.

In the area
Mara Mhor Boat Tours is located along the Corran Esplanade, Oban. This boat tour is fantastic for young and old! Skipper, Ron Stevenson, has over 29 years experience of the waters around Oban and an amazing knack for spotting dolphins, porpoises, seals and even a sea eagle or two during the boat trip. The boat was purpose built for these tours and has a spacious back deck with more than enough room for a pushchair or two and a roomy wheelhouse if it gets a little chilly on deck, there's even an electric flush toilet on board if you get caught short! Tours from 1 hour (March to October), 7 days a week, weather permitting. www.boatwildlifeoban.co.uk Tel: 01631 563387 Mobile: 07774 475995

Walk 3: Angus' Garden
Glen Lonan by Taynuilt

Angus's Garden is a hidden gem, with spectacular views over to Ben Cruachan, a secret pond to explore and a huge memorial bell to ring! This walk takes you around the garden, created by Betty MacDonald over more than 40 years in memory of her son Angus. The garden surrounds a tranquil lochan complete with ducks and swans, native and landscaped woodland, wooden bridges and boardwalks, and countless varieties of rhododendrons and azaleas, which are a spectacular sight in spring.

Despite being short and round a garden, this route is tough going as the path is very variable with unprotected drops by water edges. The land is boggy to the north of the lochan with narrow boardwalks, and there are a couple of short steep inclines. This route cannot be reversed. Two people are recommended to carry the pushchair over awkward sections. Garden open all year, 9am till dusk, entry fee (children under 16 free).

Distance:	1 mile (1.6 km)
Allow:	1 hour
Map:	Ordnance Survey 1:25 000 OL376
Grid reference:	289977

Getting there: Angus's Garden is located in Glen Lonan near the village of Taynuilt. Turn off the A85 by the Taynuilt Hotel onto the road signposted Glen Lonan. Follow this single track road for 2.5 miles and park in the Angus's Garden car park opposite Barguillean Farm.

Enter the garden by the gate house, turn right and follow the red trail. Follow the path into landscaped woodland and down 8 shallow steps. Bear round to the left, up 2 steps and continue to an immaculate (but mossy!) lawn. From the lawn, take the path to the right of the bench

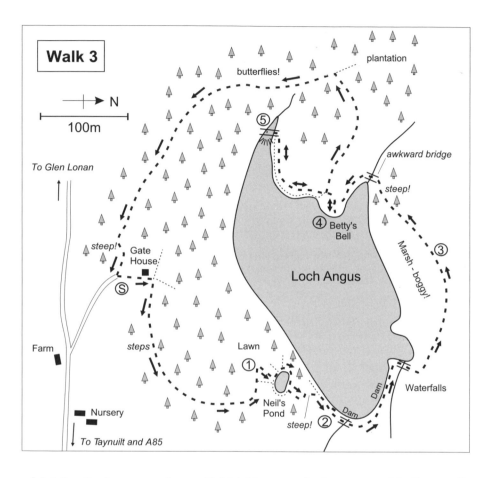

which leads down to a beautiful hidden pond – known as 'Neil's Pond', in memory of Angus' father.

1. Turn left to walk round the pond ignoring paths off to the left. Pass the bench and then turn left following an unmarked path onto a boardwalk. Continue through the trees and bear left to head steeply downhill (red posts) to the shore of Loch Angus and an abandoned boathouse.

    Look out for spectacular views of Ben Cruachan, Oban's local Munro, in the distance to your right and across the loch to the giant bell, which you will pass later in the walk.

2. Turn right to go through a gate, past the boat house and cross the reedy grass to reach a small dam. Cross the bridge in front of the dam, pass through the gate (needs lifting to open) and continue to follow the red posts.

   Walk across a larger stone dam with a small waterfall to your right, cross over 2 wooden bridges and a boardwalk. After the boardwalk bear left to make your way across the marshland to the north of Loch Angus following the sporadic red posts. Walk along the uneven path keeping the water on your left hand side. This is where it gets a little awkward as the path narrows and it can get a little boggy and uneven in places, but you can navigate through the reeds without too much difficulty, or you can carry the pushchair over the worst bits.

The path across the marsh gives you great views to the left, across the loch to the giant wind turbines in Fearnoch Forest.

3. Head towards the oak trees, looking for red trail markings on the trunks of trees ahead when you can no longer see any red posts in the ground. Continue up the hill, through the small woodland, downhill (awkward) and lift the pushchair onto a bridge with a gate.

   This bridge is awkward to access due to logs just before it, and you need to lift the gates off the supports to open them!

   Cross the bridge and continue over narrow boardwalks (slippery when wet) covering the boggy bits of the track and head uphill, turning left to emerge at a large bell.

This is Betty's Bell with Neil's Bench behind it overlooking the viewpoint, in memory of Angus' parents.

   Return to the junction and continue straight ahead along the trail,
4. bumping down some wooden steps and keeping the loch on your left following the red (and now yellow) signposts. The path at the loch shore is narrow and has an awkward camber, but you can take the higher path which is easier. Continue to a long, narrow bridge and admire the view!

The viewpoint gives you spectacular views out over Ben Cruachan, rising to over 1,126 m above sea level. The name of the mountain is properly pronounced 'kroo a hn' and the word is the battle cry of the Clan Campbell, and the Argyll and Sutherland Highlanders. Translated, it means stack, so Ben Cruachan actually means 'mountain stack', or 'stacky mountain'. This is also a good opportunity to feed the ducks!

Turn back towards the bell and, just before the steps,
5. turn left by a metal bin to join a broad track. Follow the track uphill and round to the left. At the T-junction, turn left away from the plantation and head down through lovely birch and beech woodland.

Ringing Betty's Bell!

In summer, this path has loads of butterflies! In particular, look out for Peacock Butterflies basking on the stones of the track.

Continue along the track, which has one last slog uphill! Cross the cattle grid (overgrown gate on the left) and turn left into the car park.

In the area
Inverawe Country Park and Tearoom has great nature trails, play and picnic areas for burning off excess energy and feeding the fish in the well stocked pond is great fun. The traditional smokehouse is open to the public, so you can see how the smoking is done and the café offers home baking with great views over the River Awe. Open March to December. www.inverawe-fisheries.co.uk Tel: 01866 822808

Walk 4: The Last Clansman Trail, Glen Creran, Appin

Scenic Glen Creran is the setting for this short but stunning woodland walk. The route takes in spectacular scenic views across to the mountains of the Cruachan massif and Glen Ure. The hillside is an area of regenerated woodland, where native species are slowly colonising the hillside following the removal of plantation conifers. At present, the woods are young birch, beech and oak but the feel of the wood will change over the years as it matures.

The walk follows a waymarked circular route through the woodland along stony and grassy paths that are steep in places and with unprotected drops around the route. The route can be done solo, but the bridge would be easier with two people to carry the pushchair up the steps on the way back, so you don't have to turn the pushchair on the bridge itself. Reversing the route is not recommended as the direction given avoids a steep climb.

Distance:	1.5 miles (2 km)
Allow	1 hour
Map:	OS 1:50 000 Landranger Sheet 384
Grid reference:	036488

Getting there: From the A828, turn off along the minor road to Invercreran that circuits Loch Creran. Turn along the even more minor road towards Elleric. Drive all the way to the end and park in the forestry commission car park at Elleric.

From the car park, head towards two tracks near its entrance. Take the left hand track signposted Glen Duror and Ballachulish.

1. Turn immediately left up a narrower path heading uphill, signposted Last Clansman Trail. Head uphill, steeply at first before

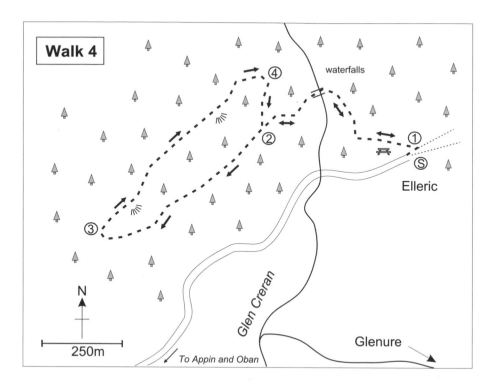

the path levels off and follows the hillside through mixed woodland. Pass a picnic bench before climbing steeply once more. The path levels off and you continue high above a rushing stream. There is a large drop to the left, so keep walking children under control. Continue to a wooden footbridge across the stream.

Go up 2 steps to cross the bridge, which spans several small waterfalls, and bump or carry the pushchair down the 8 steps on the other side.

Continue uphill along the path on the other side of the bridge past an information board.

Look out for the information boards around this route which give you details of the flora and fauna as well as the history of the Appin Murder.

2.

At the junction continue straight ahead along the level path, now grassy, ignoring a steep path to the right. Continue along as the path gently climbs through the trees.

Look out for the diverse collection of plants now growing in the woodland including ferns, mosses, bluebells, rose bay willowherb, buttercups and wood sorrel. These produce a stark contrast to the sterile forest floors found in conifer plantations.

Continue along the path as the views open out to your left.

3. Eventually, you bear round to the right and reach a bench where you can rest and admire the view.

This really is a stunning view over the valley below, with white Glenure House nestling beneath the hills of the Cruachan granite massif (Ben Cruachan is the local Munro). To the right is Loch Creran and to the left are the hills above Glen Duror, which are formed from the Ballachulish granite.

Follow the path as it contours above the trees. The path starts to drop down past more information boards to a viewpoint, with an information board about the Appin Murder.

Glenure from the Last Clansman Trail

Glenure House in the valley opposite was the home of Colin Campbell, a government factor and the victim of the infamous Appin Murder, which has been immortalised in Robert Louis Stevenson's 'Kidnapped'. Campbell (Red Fox) was shot in 1752 by a sniper in woods at Lleitir Mhor while on official business. James Stewart (James of the Glen) was arrested and tried for his involvement in the murder by a court manned mainly by Campbells. He was found guilty as an accessory, hanged at Ballachulish and his body left on the gibbet for 18 months. The murder remains unsolved but the secret of the assassin's identity is said to be kept in the Stewart family.

Continue along the path as it heads back down into woodland and past another bench.

After the bench the path drops more steeply with loose gravel (a leash is a good idea for this descent) to a hairpin bend by a large oak tree.

4. Continue down to a T-junction, where you turn left to walk back down to the footbridge. Carry or pull the pushchair up the steps, turning on the bridge (it's just wide enough!) and go down the 2 steps at the other side. Continue along the path above the stream and downhill past the picnic bench. Turn right onto the track at the bottom of the hill to return to the car park.

In the area

The Scottish Sealife Sanctuary, on the A828 two miles north of the village of Benderloch, has amazing aquaria and touch pools, with all sorts of marine animals from shrimps and starfish to sting rays, otters and sharks. You can meet rescued seals and discover how to tube-feed a seal pup! Daily talks and feeding demonstrations, café, toilets, gift shop, lochside nature trails, forest walks and an outdoor play area. Open all year, 7 days a week from 10am (except Christmas Day). Discounted tickets can be purchased in advance via the internet. www.sealsanctuary.co.uk Tel: 01631 720386

Walk 5: Beinn Lora,
Benderloch by Oban

Beinn Lora is a fantastic hill walk and the panoramic views from the viewpoint, over the Firth of Lorn to the Isle of Colonsay and beyond, make the steep parts all the more worthwhile. The viewpoint also overlooks the small Oban Airport, so on a clear day you can watch, not only the scheduled flights but the local gliders take off and land.

This is a hard-core, off-road walk through mixed conifer and broadleaf woods, past a deep gorge cut into the hillside, a beautiful waterfall and a tranquil lochan. The path is well maintained and there are some very steep inclines. The full circular route requires the pushchair to be carried over a short distance where the path narrows, so two people are needed, although this can be avoided following the alternative directions.

Distance:	3 miles (5 km)
Allow:	2 hours
Map:	OS 1:50 000 Landranger Sheet 49
Grid reference:	380905

Getting there: Beinn Lora is located in the village of Benderloch just off the A828 between North Connel and Barcaldine. Park in the Forestry Commission car park next to the petrol station, where the 405 bus from Oban also stops.

From the car park, follow the signposted trail marked by the blue posts. At the junction, turn left and follow the trail along the back of some houses, before turning round a sharp right-hand bend and heading up a steep incline. Fortunately there's a bench near the top of the hill if you want to stop and take a well-earned breather at this point! Continue along the path with dense conifer forest on your right.

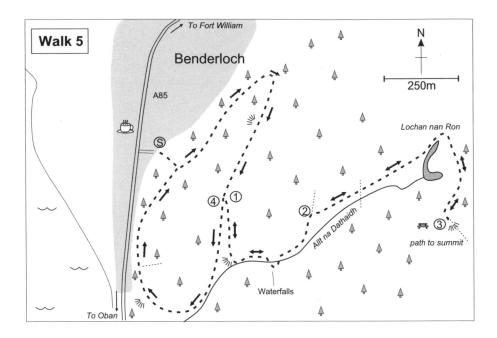

1. At the fork, keep to the left-hand path following the blue posts. Walk along the path, with the forest and then the gorge on your right hand side. Follow the path up the next steep incline, crossing over a small stream before heading up towards the waterfall.

   Watch out for the mountain bikers that frequently practices their skills on the numerous tracks down the hillside as you head up through this section of conifer forest.

2. At the signpost, follow the right-hand fork which takes you towards the Beinn Lora summit. Cross over the forestry track and follow the blue sign posts. Walk along the level path around the isolated lochan, keeping the water on your right hand side. Continue along the path until you emerge at the viewpoint and picnic bench.

   The viewpoint gives you breathtaking views out over Oban Airport, down the Firth of Lorn and even out to the Isle of Colonsay on a clear day. The path (not recommended!) continues through the gate at this point and across the heather to the trig point on Beinn Lora summit, which you can see in the distance. It's one of the best panoramic viewpoints in the southern highlands, but is too boggy and craggy at the top for pushchairs!

3. Return back down the way you came, past the lochan and gorge until you reach the junction with the red route (1).

    Look out for the mosses and lichens in the forests which are amazing at any time of year, and in spring the carpets of primrose, wood sorrel and bluebells are spectacular.

4. Turn left here and follow the red signposts down through the conifer forest until you enter a small beech wood.

    The circular route does require you to carry the pushchair for a short way, so if you want to avoid this turn right at the junction

Braving the snow on Beinn Lora!

and return back down the hill the same way you came up, following the blue posts.

Continue along the path until you pass a bench, take the next left and follow the path down-hill keeping the fence on your left. This is where it gets a little awkward as the path narrows and is stepped with tree roots and rocks, but can be navigated if you carry the pushchair for half a dozen steps.

The beech trees are huge and incredibly knarled, and often remind me of Treebeard and the Ents in Lord of the Rings!

Continue along the path down the hill until you reach a junction at the bottom, turn left and simply follow the path back to the car park.

In the area
Tralee Bay is one of the best sandy beaches in the Argyll area and is off the A828 just north of the village of Benderloch, where this walk starts, signposted for Tralee and South Shian. Foot access is via a vehicle track (OS 391900), park in the layby opposite track entrance.

Walk 6: Sailean Lime Kilns, Lismore, Firth of Lorn

If you didn't know Lismore was there, you'd easily overlook this low-lying island (literally!) north-west of Oban, but it is a gem of a place and well worth a visit. This limestone island is incredibly fertile and the wild flowers in the verges are spectacular in spring.

This walk takes you through agricultural land, past a beautiful bay at Sailean and an old lime works, complete with kilns, quarrymen's cottages and quay (all now in ruins unfortunately). The path is well maintained and there are some fairly steep inclines. The full circular route is fine for just one person, but remember to take the wellies if it's been raining in the last couple of days. This walk can be done as a foot passenger from the Oban ferry, just make sure you allow enough time to make the return crossing!

Distance:	4.5 miles (7 km)
Allow:	3 hours
Map:	OS 1:50 000 Landranger Sheet 49
Grid reference:	408853

Getting there: The island of Lismore is located to the north-west of Oban and can be reached by ferry (Oban to Achnacroish) in approximately 50 minutes.

From the ferry terminal at Achnacroish, follow the road straight up the hill, passing the primary school on your left.

1. At the junction, turn left on to the 'main' road (B8045), signposted for Achinduin and follow the road for approximately 500 metres before turning right at the next junction. Continue along this road through open farmland for about 1 mile (1.5 km).

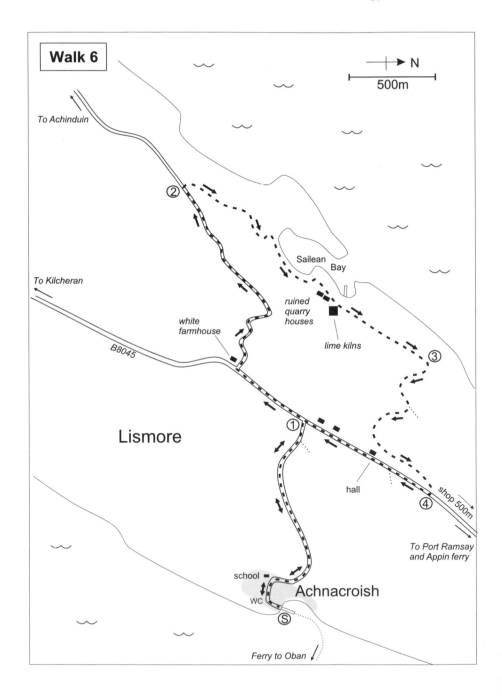

Walk 6

→ N

500m

To Achinduin

②

Sailean Bay

ruined quarry houses

white farmhouse

lime kilns

③

To Kilcheran

B8045

①

Lismore

hall

shop 500m

④

To Port Ramsay and Appin ferry

school

WC

Achnacroish

Ⓢ

Ferry to Oban ↘

Lismore is unusual geologically as it consists of limestone, which isn't a common rock in this area. This has produced fertile soils, and the name Lismore is derived from the Gaelic 'Lios Mor' which means Big Garden. The island sits on the line of the Great Glen Fault and its inhabitants are used to the odd tremor as the fault continues to move.

2. Turn right onto a rough vehicle track marked to Sailean. Follow the track up a gentle incline before an equally gentle descent to the sea. Follow the track northwards along the coast (at this point it may get a little boggy if it's been raining or if the tide is particularly high), past the old lime kilns, quarrymen's cottages and quay.

This point offers fantastic views over the Firth of Lorn to the forbidding, but beautiful granite hills of the Morvern Peninsula beyond. Watch out for oyster catchers, herons and, if you're lucky, otters feasting on mackerel when you reach the bay at the foot of the hill.

The Morvern hills from the main road on Lismore

3. After about a mile (1.5 km) the track turns inland. Continue to follow the track and pass through a farm gate.

Commercial lime kilns were established on the island in the early 1800s and the largest at Sailean survived until 1934. At the peak of the industry, there were 24 local boats regularly carrying lime to Glasgow.

4. When you reach the next junction turn right to rejoin the main road.

If you turn left here, there's a shop selling snacks and ice-cream a further 500 metres along the road.

Continue along the main road, turn left at the junction signposted to Achnacroish and return down the hill to the ferry slipway.

In the area

Lismore Museum and Heritage Centre offers a fantastic insight into how folk have lived their lives on a small Scottish island from the earliest evidence, dating back to 3500 BC, right up to the present day. There's also a great café! Open April to October and museum oprn by arrangement from November to March. www.isleoflismore.com Tel: 01631 760030

Walk 7: Kerrera and Gylen Castle, by Oban

The island of Kerrera sits just across the water from Oban. Once a major ferry hub for passengers travelling from Mull and the Hebrides to the mainland, it is now a tranquil island served by passenger ferry; the only cars you'll encounter are those of the island's residents.

This walk is a loop of the southern half of the island, taking in views of the mainland at first and then across to Mull as you head around the island's southern tip. At the half way point there is the option to take a short detour to Gylen Castle, and of course there's the Tea Garden, open from Easter to September. There are some steep and prolonged inclines, but you can always just head back from the tea shop to avoid these.

N.B. If the café is closed there is no shelter on this walk. It is essential that you take waterproofs and food and allow enough time to catch the return ferry.

Distance:	6 miles (10 km)
Allow:	4 hours
Map:	Ordnance Survey 1:25 000 OL359
Grid reference:	830287

Getting there: From Oban, follow the signs past the Oban ferry terminal towards Gallanach. Park at Kerrera Ferry and take the passenger boat across to the island (fee). Times available from Caledonian MacBrayne.

From the landing slip, walk uphill towards the phone box and buildings and turn left to follow a broad gravel track.

From the track you get a great view of the old sea cliffs on the other side of Kerrera Sound, a relic of when sea level was higher than it is today.

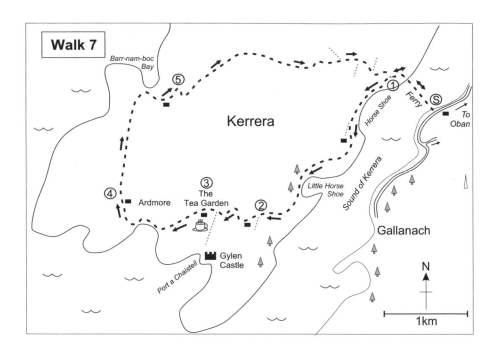

1. Take the left fork to head slightly downhill and along the coast, with the sea on your left. Go through the gate towards Ardchoirc Farm – put dogs on leads here! Fork left to continue around the coast past a row of white cottages. Go through a second gate and follow the path as it winds uphill. Pass a bench and go through a third gateway before heading inland towards a white house.

2.
   At the fork turn right to go further inland signposted 'Gylen Castle, Tea Garden and Bunkhouse'. Go steeply uphill past the white house and follow the track round to the right. Head downhill along the track towards a house with views of the Isle of Mull across the water.

   To detour to the castle, turn left through a metal gate signposted 'Gylen Castle' and join a grassy path. Go through a second gate and along the bottom of the cliffs to the bay. Return to the track and turn left to continue the walk.

Gylen Castle, built in 1562, is high above you on the rocky promontory. During its occupation, the bay was a ferry port and the main access was via boat. The castle is a fortified tower house built in the Scots Baronial style by the MacDougalls. It had four storeys, two turrets and the walls today stand nearly at their full height. The castle was besieged in 1647, at the end of which it was ransacked, set on fire and it has been a ruin ever since.

3. Pass the Tea Garden (amazing cakes and scones!), go through a gate and continue along the track. The track curves round to meet the coast where you go through another gate and start to head downhill.

Out to sea is Seil Island straight ahead of you, with the heights of Lunga beyond and the Garvellachs to the right. The rocks here are knobbly Devonian conglomerates, deposited in rivers, unconformably overlain by smooth looking Lorne Lavas, relics of major volcanic eruptions around 300 million years ago!

Admiring Gylen Castle

Head downhill towards the cliffs of Mull across the water.

4. Ford a stream and pass a small house before heading round to the right to join a rough track. Cross a small stream and head steeply uphill.

   This stretch is muddy with loose rocks but this is the worst terrain you'll encounter today!

   Pass a pond just before the top and as you start heading downhill there are lovely views ahead to Lismore and its lighthouse. The going gets easier now as you ford a small stream to head along a grassy track and through a gate. Pass a pond (ducks!) and continue between the coast on your left and old sea cliffs on your right – look out for basking seals and passing ferries! Contour round to the right and head downhill towards a white house.

5. Drop down to the house and continue straight ahead to climb the very steep(!), metalled road up the hill. From the top you get fantastic views across to the mountains of the Cruachan massif in the distance. Keep going along the undulating road and through two gates, with views across to Oban. Go through a gate at a T-junction and turn right. At the farm go straight on through a wooden gate and continue downhill, through yet another gate and past the old school. Carry on straight ahead all the way back down to the ferry slip.

In the area
Kerrera Tea Garden, located just north of Gylen Castle, offers great range of home made food and fair trade drinks, all served in either a wonderful garden or byre depending on the weather! Open April to September. www.kerrerabunkhouse.co.uk Tel: 01631 570223

Walk 8: Easdale Island, by Oban

The island of Easdale, just off the coast of Seil Island, is famous for its slate. Now disused, the quarries provide a dramatic reminder of the once busy industry on this and the neighbouring islands of Seil, Belnahua and Luing. Quarrying started in the 1600s and continued until the late 1800s, when work was dramatically reduced after the Great Storm flooded the quarries. The last slate was cut in the 1950s.

This walk follows the path around the edge of the island following old tramways and narrow footpaths, ending up in the village, which consists of picturesque single storey, white cottages built for the quarry workers. The paths are narrow in places, but the blackberries are delicious!! Pub, café and museum on the island in season, pub and toilets in Ellenabeich.

Distance: 1.25 miles (2 km)
Allow: 1 hour (excluding ferry)
Map: Ordnance Survey 1:25 000 OL359
Grid reference: 741174

Getting there: From the A816 south of Oban, turn off at Kilninver, signposted Easdale. Take the single track road over the Atlantic Bridge and across Seil Island, turning right at junctions to follow the main road and signs to Easdale. Park in the public car park at the end of the road in Ellenabeich.

Take the passenger ferry from Ellenabeich (small fee, break over lunch). There is room for a pushchair, but you may need to fold it during busy times.

1. Once on the island, walk up the slipway, past the phone box and turn right along the track past the village hall on your left.

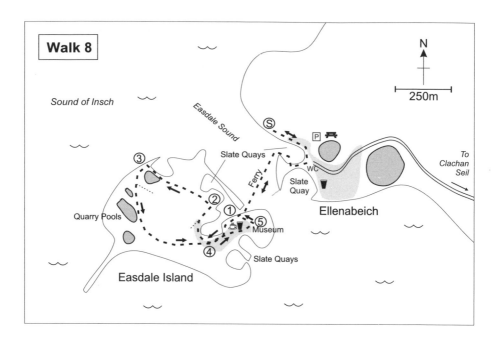

Built in 2003 on the site of the old Drill Hall, the hall hosts concerts, plays, films and other diverse events throughout the year.

Continue past the square, surrounded by white cottages (the Shieling) and follow the track round to the right past the harbour and houses.

Most of the cottages were built to house the quarry workers and their families. Many still belong to their descendents, and the island has around 70 permanent residents, making it the most densely populated Scottish island! The cottages had 'detached' vegetable gardens located just below the hill (124 ft high!), with topsoil imported from Ireland to enable the community to grow their own produce.

2. After the last house bear left to continue along the grassy track. Continue past the slate waste heaps, a remnant from the island's quarrying days, and through the 'walls' between the heaps.

 Cross the narrow causeway between two quarry pools, keeping walking children under strict control and watching out for uneven ground as the fences are not very strong.

To your right you can see the island of Insh and the Lismore lighthouse. Ahead you get a stunning view of Mull with the high peaks of Ben Mor and neighbouring hills behind the steep cliffs. Look out for ferries, yachts and kayaks on the water.

3. Follow the path round to the left and uphill, taking the lower path furthest from the pool edge, and continue between the fencing. Bear left, dropping down by a slate heap towards ruined quarry buildings. Ignore a steep narrow path up to the viewpoint (worth the climb if you come back without the pushchair) and continue along past two quarry pools on your right (look out for swimmers in summer!).

   Keep following the path as it swings left around the end of the island. Continue along the path which narrows and gets awkward in places. A leash on the pushchair is recommended as there is a drop to the left at the most awkward point.

Snow on Mull from Easdale Island

This stretch is vegetated in summer, but still passable and the blackberries are delicious! Follow the path through a pair of high walls to return to the houses. Look out for small paths to your right, leading to viewpoints and small stony coves, lovely for practising stone skimming.

4. Turn left just before a wire fence to join the track into the village. Turn right and cross the Shieling towards the far corner and past the Folk Museum on your right (well worth a visit) to a viewpoint by yet more quarry pools with a lovely view over to 'mainland' Seil.

The quarry pool here is the site of the International Stone Skimming Championships held every September.

Return to the Shieling and past the waymarker with international mileages. Turn right by the signpost and pass (or go into!) the Puffer Bar on your left. Turn left between a white cottage and the taller old school to return to the track.

The house on your right was once the island school. Now children have a daily commute by ferry to the primary school at Ellenabeich – interesting and very wet in winter!

5. Turn right to return to the ferry, or left to visit the tea room (in season) and play area before you leave.

In the area

Sea Fari Adventures, based in the harbour area on Seil Island (next to the Easdale ferry slipway), offer a totally unique wildlife experience. Tours combine the pure exhilaration of a fast boat ride with the thrill of close encounters with Scotland's magnificent sealife and scenery, including basking sharks, minke whales, sea eagles and the chance to visit the Gulf Of Corryvreckan, home to the world's third largest whirlpool. Seats in the front of the boat are specially adapted for parents and children and they are happy to take children over the age of 4. Under 4's are carried at the discretion of the skipper depending on weather conditions, so it's probably best to give them a call before setting out. Tours run from March to October. www.seafari.co.uk Tel: 01852 300003

Walk 9: Torosay Castle, Craignure, Mull

Craignure port on the east coast of Mull boasts two local castles, Duart and Torosay. This walk takes you from the ferry port to Torosay Castle with lovely views across the bay to Duart Castle. The gardens and castle are open to the public (fee) and have a café and children's playground. To add extra fun, the Mull Light Railway runs between the start and end of this walk, so in season you have the option of returning by train!

The walk follows a gravel track through woodland with sea views and there are moderate inclines. The castle gardens have several sets of steps which are not all avoidable. This walk can be done on foot from the Oban Ferry.

Distance:	2.5 miles (4 km)
Allow:	1 hour 30 minutes
Map:	Ordnance Survey 1:25 000 OL375
Grid reference:	718371

Getting there: Park by the quay in Craignure (there is more parking by the pub and village hall), or start on foot from the Oban Ferry.

From the quay, turn left and walk along the pavement past the tourist information office. Join the path through the picnic area and continue past the pub, village hall and garage.

1. About 100m after the garage, turn left by Torosay North Lodge to join a track through woodland on the Torosay Castle Estate. Head uphill to a junction where you bear left to continue straight ahead on the level (not up to the radio masts).

   To your left, you now get a great view across the sea to Morvern on the mainland and the Isand of Lismore, and below you may see the steam from the trains on the railway.

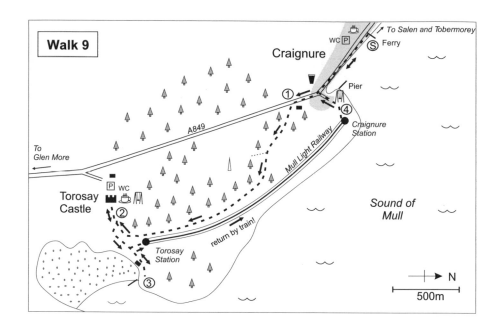

Go through a gateway and head back into woodland, past Fenella's Wood on your right.

This is an area planted with endangered tree species from Chile! The area was cleared of Sitka Spruce and now contains trees including the Chilean Cedar, Monkey Puzzle and Southern Beech.

Head downhill with lovely sea views to your left, past a picnic table. There are large cliffs here which are poorly protected.

You get your first view of Duart Castle here, on the headland across the bay.

Continue along the track through the trees and head downhill, with the railway below you. Carry on above the station building and as the track heads round to the right, Torosay Castle comes into view.

2. Go through the car park to access the castle and gardens (toilets, tea room, playground).

The castle and gardens are worth visiting (fee). The castle is a family home dating from 1856 and is a fine example of the Scottish Baronial style by architect David Bryce. The gardens cover 12 acres and are attributed to Robert Lorimar. They include grand terraces, a statue walk, walled garden, Japanese garden and bog garden. There are steps, which are not all avoidable.

Return to the car park and head right, downhill on the track towards the bay. Follow the track around to the left, past the turning to the railway. Continue to the white cottage and the bay where you have a fantastic view across to Duart Castle.

This is a lovely sandy bay and good for a break, but bear in mind that the picnic tables are for the use of the cottages! Ahead there is a war memorial with good views back up the coast, but steps to access it.

3. Return to the railway, and turn right to take the train back to Craignure (April-October). Alternatively, go back to the car park

Relaxing in Torosay Castle Gardens

and turn right to return the way you came, along the woodland track back to the village, remembering to call at the playground on your way!

4. From Craignure station, take the track downhill and through the campsite. Go past the playground (which is great!) and village hall to the road.

Just outside the police station are two standing stones. These are the Penny Gate Stones that once stood at the end of Craignure east pier, built in 1853 by one of the lighthouse-building Stevensons. They were used as part of a toll gate at the end of the pier and a penny was taken from anyone who wanted to visit the island.

Turn right onto the road and follow the pavement back to the quay.

In the area
The Isle of Mull Railway was opened in 1984 and each year over 25,000 passengers make the journey from Craignure to the beautiful Torosay Castle. The carriages are pulled by either miniature steam or diesel engines (almost straight out of 'Thomas the Tank Engine'!) and the journey takes about 25 minutes. Trains run April to October and are a perfect end to this walk!
www.mullrail.co.uk Tel: 01680 812494

Walk 10: Clach Thoull, Port Appin

This is a level walk around a beautiful headland below sea cliffs, which were formed when sea level was higher than it is today. At the end of the headland you are rewarded not only with stunning views over the sea and the Island of Lismore, but by two old sea arches, now stranded several metres above the water. Not only that, but there's a great view of Castle Stalker as you drive to the car park!

The track is good most of the way, but there is a section of about 300m of narrow and wet woodland path before you meet the road. However, the walk to the headland and back is well worth doing if you don't fancy the woodland path. The whole route can be done with a double off-road pushchair.

Distance:	1.5 miles (2.5 km)
Allow:	1 hour
Map:	Ordnance Survey 1:25 000 OL376
Grid reference:	904453

Getting there: Turn off the A828 by the garage in Appin, signposted to Port Appin (Castle Stalker to your right!). Go through the village and park in the car park above the pier. Toilets.

From the car park, follow the signposted track between two white houses. Head along between the houses, the last two of which have turrets! Carry on along the track under the cliffs with lovely views over to Lismore, Morvern and Mull.

To your left all along this walk you can see the old sea cliffs. Sea level is not constant and has gone up and down repeatedly during geological time and at present is actually very low. These cliffs were formed when sea level was just a few metres higher than present. This could either be because actual sea level has gone down, or because the land has rebounded up since the glaciers retreated after the last ice age. Do this walk before

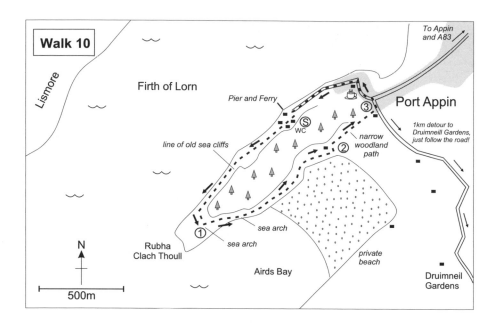

Walk 10

Lismore

Firth of Lorn

Pier and Ferry

To Appin and A83

Port Appin

S WC

1km detour to Druimneill Gardens, just follow the road!

line of old sea cliffs

narrow woodland path

②

③

sea arch

sea arch

N

500m

Rubha Clach Thoull

Airds Bay

private beach

①

Druimneil Gardens

the effects man is having on rising sea levels make them sea cliffs once again!

Keep following the track, past a small pebbly beach to a gate. Go through the gate and just continue along the track until you reach the headland, where there is a bench to admire the view. As you reach the bench, the first sea arch, Clach Thoull, appears.

The headland is called Rubha Clach Thoull which means 'point of the holey rock', referring to the sea arch, now stranded on land. You can walk through the arch, but it's a bit rough for a pushchair, especially down the other side (though I have to admit ours went through it!).

1. Follow the track around the arch and continue to the other side of the headland, which is slightly more sheltered and wooded. Look out for the second smaller arch, hidden in the trees to your left and also the small sea caves.

    The rock here is quartzite, metamorphosed sandstone, and here it has a lovely white, sugary texture – just like Kendal mint cake!

Clach Thoull, now definitely above sea level!

Continue along the track beside Airds Bay until you reach a white house, where the track ends.

2. Go in front of the house and through a small metal gate marked 'Footpath to Port Appin'. This brings you to a narrow path through the woods which is awkward in places and can be muddy. Cross a drainage ditch and follow the path for about 300 m until you come to a house.

3. By the house, go through the gate and join the road for easy going once more. Turn left and then left at the T-junction to walk back into Port Appin. Pause at the lighthouse exhibition by the village hall for information on the village and surrounding area.

The building housing the exhibition was originally the light chamber for the lighthouse you can see just offshore. When demolition was threatened, the locals painted the lighthouse as 'Mr Blobby' – pink with yellow spots!! Then the lighthouse board came and painted it white again and the locals then painted it yellow with pink spots. This caused much hilarity, but unfortunately it didn't stop the lighthouse board exchanging the structure for the more modern version that is there today.

Follow the road back to the pier and the car park.

The village has a shop, post office and craft shop which sells toys and takeaway tea and coffee! There's also a seafood restaurant by the pier.

In the area
Lismore Ferry (www.isleoflismore.com) carries only passengers and operates between Port Appin and Point at the north end of the island all year round. The journey is approximately 10 minutes. Bicycles are carried for free on the ferry and can be hired from either Lismore (01631 760 213), where they meet you off the boat, or Port Appin Bike Hire (01631 730 391).

Walk 11: Jubilee Bridge, Appin

The Jubilee Bridge is a narrow wooden bridge crossing the tidal estuary between Appin and Portnacroish. Though it looks rickety, the bridge is solid and little ones just love walking over it! Not only is it fun, but it affords one of the best views of Castle Stalker - a picturesque 15th century castle sat on an island. It is one of the most photographed castles in Scotland and features in Monty Python's 'Holy Grail'.

This is a level walk along the old Ballachulish railway, now a multi-user trail, and across boardwalks and gravel paths. To add a bit of extra excitement, the boardwalks are too narrow for your back wheels and you have to perfect the art of 'wheelbarrowing' your pushchair resting only on the front wheel! Needless to say, this walk is for 3-wheelers only and walking children need to kept under control around tidal pools.

Please note: At high tides, the section from the boardwalks to the road beyond the bridge can flood and there is the possibility of being stranded on the bridge. Check tide times before you leave.

Distance:	2.2 miles (3.5 km)
Allow:	1 hour 30 minutes
Map:	Ordnance Survey 1:25 000 OL376
Grid reference:	936463

Getting there: From the A828 between Oban and Fort William turn off towards Port Appin. Go past the fire station and take the second right and park in the car park by the school. If the car park is full, park on the road.

From the car park, take the gravel path at its far end, go through the gateway and join the old railway line at a T-junction.

1. Turn left and walk along the metalled track. Pass the school and its access bridge (look closely at the bridge posts!) and continue

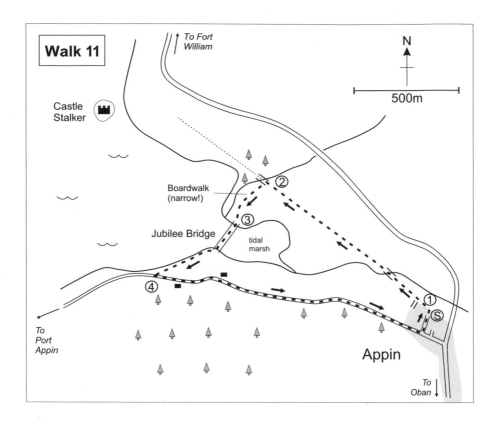

along the track. Cross a stream and go through the gateway at the far end of the bridge (if the main gate is shut there is a small gate to its left).

As you walk along you start to get views of the wooden Jubilee Bridge crossing the estuary ahead of you.

2. Just before the second bridge, turn steeply down to the left and go through a metal gate. Turn left and walk along a narrow gravel path which runs alongside a stream.
    Follow the path through the reed beds. Pass a gate and bridge on your right (do not cross) and keep following the path as it bends round to the left until it meets the boardwalk.
    Join the boardwalk, and wheelbarrow along the wooden boards.

This is a classic off-roading technique, and the advantage of this boardwalk is that it's narrow enough to sit the wheels either side of the boards if you want a rest! Keep an eye on walking children, especially crossing over water as there is no protection on the sides of the boardwalk.

3. The boardwalk continues to the bridge, where you will be relieved to be able to push normally! Go onto the bridge for spectacular views of Castle Stalker, with the hills of Morvern in the background, and up the glen towards the mountains above Glen Creran.

There has been a castle on the island since the early 1300s, but the present Castle Stalker dates from the 1440s. It has passed between the Stewarts and Campbells several times through battles, sieges and drunken bets! It was inhabited until about 1800 when the Campbells moved to Airds House, after which it fell into ruin. The final exchange was in 1908 when it was bought by Charles Stewart of Achara from the

Castle Stalker from Jubilee Bridge

Campbells. He and his successors renovated the castle to a habitable state and live in it today.

Cross the bridge, and wheelbarrow for a few metres on the other side, to bear right past a boat and join a narrow gravel path along the shore. Pass the houses and follow the path all the way to the road.

4. Turn left onto the road and follow it all the way back to Appin, looking out for traffic. Turn left by the fire station and return to your car.

In the area

Castle Stalker View Café and Gift Shop has one of the best views from any café on the west coast of Scotland! Looking out over Castle Stalker to the island of Lismore, Loch Linnhe and the Morvern Hills beyond, the café serves great home-made food to complement the view. Definitely worth stopping for lunch if you're driving between Oban and Fort William. Open March to December. www.castlestalkerview.co.uk Tel: 01631 730444

Walk 12: Ardgour Lochans, North Corran

Ardgour is a rugged peninsula on the western side of Loch Linnhe and the Great Glen Fault. Though virtually surrounded by water, it is easily accessible from Fort William via the Corran Ferry. The headland at Corran is comparatively flat, and is the site of one of the oldest trade routes in the Highlands as well as a cute Stevenson lighthouse.

This is a lovely woodland walk, which takes you around two lochans on good tracks and metalled roads, with fabulous views up to the mountains behind Fort William and down to Loch Linnhe and the coast. The paths on the route are suitable for double off-roaders. As the walk starts from the ferry, it is not necessary to take the car over, and there are three possible pubs to visit – two on the walk and one at the ferry!

Distance: 2.5 miles (4 km)
Allow: 1 hour 30 mins
Map: Ordnance Survey 1:25 000 OL391
Grid reference: 015637

Getting there: Take the Corran Ferry off the A828 just south of Fort William (fee for cars, free for foot passengers) – you can park on either side of the water.

From the ferry pier, turn right to walk along the road past the Inn at Ardgour with the sea on your right.

You have just crossed Loch Linnhe which sits on the Great Glen Fault, a large strike-slip fault where the earths plates slide past each other (like the San Andreas Fault in California). The rocks on this side have moved hundreds of miles south-west and are markedly different and significantly older than those just across the water.

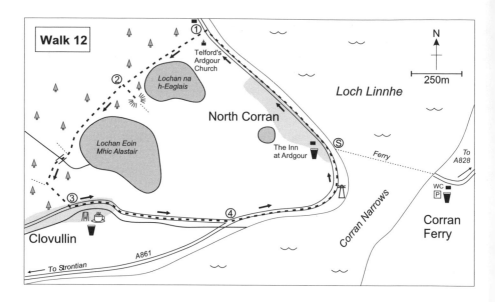

Pass a playground on your left and continue past the end of the houses to Ardgour Parish Church.

The church was built in 1829 and was designed by the engineer Thomas Telford, one of forty-two in the highlands that were part of a parliamentary initiative for the Church of Scotland.

1. Just after the church, turn left up a stony track into woodland. After about 100 m you get to Lochan na-h Eaglais (Church Lochan) which can be seen through the trees. Continue along the track (no access to the water) to the end of the lochan. To get a great view of both lochans, turn left at the end of the lochan to walk a short distance down a path until the trees open out.

   The lochans in this area are kettle holes, which are hollows formed during glacial ice melting at the end of the last ice age.

2. Return to the main track and continue past Lochan Eoian Mhic Alastair (Ewan McAlastair's Lochan), which can again be seen through the trees to your left. Continue to the end of the lochan and follow the main track ignoring a turning to your right.

Cross over a stone bridge and follow the track around to the left through rhodedendrons.

At the next T-junction, turn left to join a metalled lane, which is the drive for Ardgour House. Walk down the drive to join the road at the next T-junction.

3. Turn left onto the road and walk through the village, Clovullin, which consists of a collection of crofts. Opposite the junction is the shop and licensed tea room if you fancy a break! Follow the road past the school and beside a small stream until you reach the main road.

4. Turn left onto the main road and walk along the verge. This road can get busy and is fast, so watch out for traffic. There are lovely views down Loch Linnhe here and a beach! It's awkward to get the pushchair onto the beach, but can be managed by two people.

Thomas Telford's Ardgour Church

Continue to Ardgour lighthouse, which marks the west side of the Corran Narrows.

The narrows are one of the oldest trade routes in the Highlands. Cattle were swum across the loch here, on their way to market. The lighthouse was built by David and Thomas Stevenson and dates from 1860.

Pass the lighthouse and the ferry queuing bay, where there are information boards. Continue along the pavement back to the pub, the ferry and your car.

In the area
Phoenix Nursery Soft Play Centre can be found at the Nevis Centre in Fort William. This is the largest soft play in Argyll and Lochaber and offers a great opportunity to burn off some energy if it's wet outside. The centre has a ball pond, cargo net, bouncy castle, walkway train, tunnels, monster maze, slides and chutes. Under 5s soft play area and café also available. Open all year round.
www.neviscentre.co.uk Tel: 01397 700721

Walk 13: Ariundle Oakwoods, Strontian

Ariundle is a fragment of the native woodland that once covered much of this area and even much of Britain. The trees are dominated by oaks with holly, hazel, birch, rowan, and willows, all of which suit the thin acid soil on top of the granite bedrock. It is a stunningly beautiful place with spring flowers, 250 different mosses, rare butterflies, abundant birdlife, and resident mammals include the pine marten and wild cat.

This walk follows a waymarked trail along gravel and grassy paths, with a stretch of boardwalk just wide enough for a pushchair! There are two narrow squeezes, and if you have a wide pushchair you may need to either remove the wheels (if practical) or lift, but otherwise the going is good. Dogs must be kept on a lead in the nature reserve.

Distance: 2.2 miles (3.5 km)
Allow: 1 hour 30 mins
Map: Ordnance Survey 1:25 000 OL391
Grid reference: 826633

Getting there: From Strontian turn up the road to Polloch. Turn right past the café, signposted Ariundle and park in the forestry car park.

From the car park, walk along the forest track signposted Airgh Fhionnaidl. Go past the first path to the right (bridleway with a large deep ford!!!) and continue along the track to the second turning on the right marked by a footprint.

1. Turn right onto the narrow woodland path and between a boulder and a tree (you may need to remove wheels or lift here if you have a wide pushchair) and follow the path past an information board to the river.

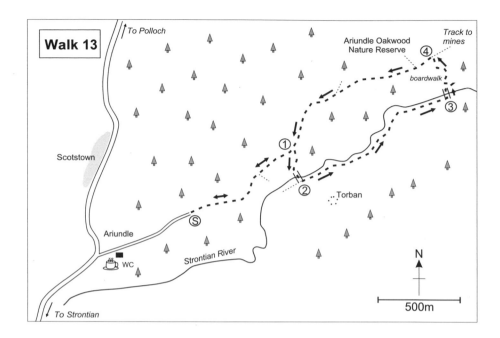

Go over the bridge and turn left between two boulders (narrow and rocky).

The boulders here are made of granite, which forms the bedrock in this area, and have been rounded by ice and water action. The granite produces thin acidic soils which many plants can't tolerate.

2. Follow the path, with lovely views down the valley, over a small wooden bridge and continue along the now grassy path alongside the river. Pause at the information board.

On the hill above you is Torban, a settlement belonging to Clan Cameron. The people lived in turf-topped houses, remains of which can be seen on the hillside. They kept cattle and grew crops; the traces of strip-farming can still be seen on the ground. The settlement was abandoned in the 19th century.

Cross an awkward drainage ditch and a second small wooden bridge. As the path becomes gravel once more, you can see the bridge over the river in the distance. Go up a short steep section and drop down to the bridge.

Just before the bridge is a small boardwalk to the right leading to a bench with a view!

3. Cross the bridge and turn right along the path through Scot's pine and young birch trees. Turn left onto the boardwalk and follow it as it zig-zags across the marshy section into the nature reserve. Dogs must be kept on a lead!

   At the end of the boardwalk, continue up the gravel path until it reaches the forest track.

Turn left onto the track and go over a wooden bridge.

Up to your right are the Ariundle Oakwoods. These are a remnant of an ancient oakwood, which stretched along the Atlantic coast in Britain. They were cleared for farming and timber, with only a few scattered remnants still surviving, such as here and in North Wales. The trees and boulders are covered in abundant mosses and lichens, and the woods are home to a variety of wildlife, including rare species such as the wild cat.

Bridge at Ariundle

4. Go past a right turn to the woodland walk (lovely but not suitable for push-

chairs!) and just continue along the track, past several information boards. As you leave the nature reserve, simply follow the track all the way back to the car park.

More information can be found at the Visitor Centre and café at the road junction.

In the area
Ardnamurchan Lighthouse and Visitor Centre is located at the most westerly point of the British mainland. The more adventurous can climb to the top of the lighthouse (height of 36 m via 152 steps and two ladders!) for fantastic views to the Hebridean Isles of Skye, Muck, Eigg and Rhum. Tours every half hour from 11 am - 4.30 pm (April to October) and must be booked in advance. There is also an exhibition centre explaining the operation and history of the lighthouse and a chance to learn how the huge foghorn operated and was kept in good working order. Coffee shop open 5 days a week throughout the season and a grassy walled enclosure next to the coffee shop terrace provides a safe place to burn off some energy.
 www.ardnamurchanlighthouse.com Tel: 01972 510210

Walk 14: Woodland Walk, Arisaig

Arisaig is a picturesque village on the Road to the Isles, with a sweeping harbour, views to Skye and the Small Isles, and fantastic sunsets! The coast here once housed a thriving community of crofters and fishermen, but this area was a victim of the Highland Clearances in the early 1800s, when whole communities were evicted to make way for more profitable sheep. The ruins of their crofts can still be seen.

This is a lovely walk around woodland and coast, along good tracks and quiet lanes with some steep inclines. The village has a selection of shops, a pub, cafés, a good children's playground and an exhibition on the history of the village. The walk is suitable for double off-roaders.

Distance:	3 miles (5 km)
Allow:	1 hour 30 mins
Map:	Ordnance Survey 1:25 000 OL398
Grid reference:	658864

Getting there: Arisaig is located just off the A830 Road to the Isles south of Mallaig. Turn off the bypass and park in the centre of the village by the harbour.

From the centre of Arisaig, walk along past the shops with the harbour on your right. Go past the Sea and Islands Centre and walk along the road.

Built on the site of an old smiddy, the Sea and Islands Centre houses an exhibition on the history and life in Arisaig and the Islands. There is an information board here with a map of walks from the town.

1. Turn right down the road signposted Rhu. Drag your children past the playground (you come back this way!) and go across the bridge over the Canal.

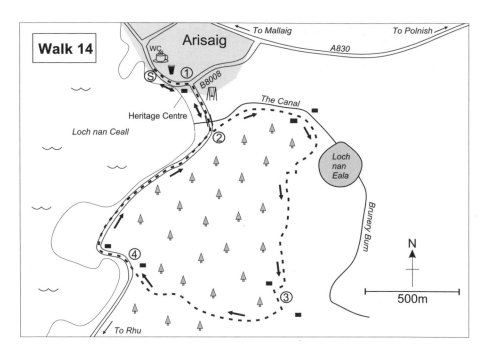

There are lovely views out to sea to the islands of Eigg and Rhum, known as the Small Isles.

2. Turn left just before the 'children playing' sign and cross the cattle grid to walk up a track with the canal on your left. Walk through lovely mature deciduous trees and past a reed bed. Continue along the track as it bends around to the right and pass the barns.

Look out for Highland cattle!

Go through a gate into a field and follow the track around to the right with Loch nan Eala on your left and wooded hillside on your right. Keep following the track, rougher now, ignoring a driveway to a white cottage. Continue to a cross-roads just before a second white house.

3. Turn right at the cross-roads to head slightly uphill and carry on over a cattle grid. Cross the driveway to the big house and drop back downhill to the metalled lane.

4. Turn right to continue straight ahead and walk along the coast road, looking out for cars.

There are yellow flag irises on the marsh beds in summer and blackberries in the hedgerows in autumn. The rhodedendrons are garden escapees!

Woodland by The Canal

Continue along the lane, round a sharp right hand bend and pass a new house, head uphill and back down the other side. Return to the bridge over the canal and walk back to the playground at the junction. Turn left to return to the centre of Arisaig and your car.

In the area
The Silver Sands of Morar is the name given to the old coast road which runs from Arisaig north to Morar. This stretch of coastline is renowned for its breathtaking white sandy beaches, turquoise waters and unbeatable views across to the isles of Eigg and Muck and further north to Skye. At Portnaluchaig, the road skirts the beach itself, and it's definitely worth parking the car and exploring the beaches and islets of the bay. Another good stopping place is a little further north at Camusdarach, from where a path leads to the magnificent dunes lining this part of the coastline.

Walk 15: Fassfern Woodland, Glenfinnan

Fassfern woodland is a privately managed plantation forest dating back to the 1950s. It forms part of the Fassfern Estate, famously visited by Bonnie Prince Charlie in 1745 and is said to be where he picked a white rose, which later became his symbol. The forest is managed with environmental considerations in mind and has won awards for environmentally sustainable forestry. As this is a working forest, please obey all warning signs and note that paths can be closed at times.

This is a lovely, varied waymarked walk through forest, clearings and past hidden lochans. There are spectacular views to Ben Nevis (on a clear day!) and down to Loch Eil. All paths are good, though they are grassy and wet in places and there is, unfortunately, one locked gate to lift the pushchair over. The car park has a picnic and barbecue area.

Distance:	1.5 miles (2.3 km)
Allow:	1 hour
Map:	Ordnance Survey 1:25 000 OL391
Grid reference:	020789

Getting there: Fassfern is signposted from the A830 'Road to the Isles' between Fort William and Glenfinnan. Follow the loop road round until you see a poorly signposted car park by a bridge and a cottage (on the right as you head from Fort William).

From the car park, head across the grass towards a small gate in a wall, marked Ceunn gun an Lochan. Go through the gate and follow the gravel path and boardwalk through the young birch trees, crossing a couple of drainage ditches on your way.

1. At a T-junction turn right to follow the red waymarked path slightly uphill through mixed woodland.

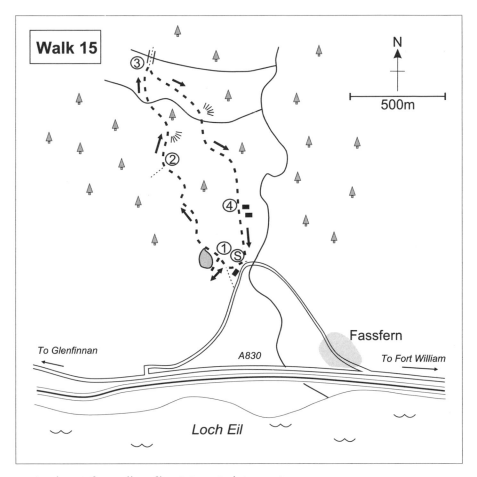

Look out for yellow flag irises in late spring.

Detour left to visit the woodland lochan (benches). Return to the track and turn left to continue uphill and cross a causeway between the lochan on your left and a lovely reed bed on your right.

Pass another red post and continue uphill along the track which bends round gently to the left.

As you climb remember to look back at the views. Loch Eil comes into view in the valley below and to the left is Ben Nevis and its neighbouring hills.

Small boy and big mountain! Ben Nevis as seen from Fassfern

The path levels off by a marsh (with buttercups and orchids) and you head towards a gate, which is locked. Lift over the gate and enter the woodland to continue along a grassy path.

2. At the next junction, marked by two red posts, turn right to continue uphill through a young plantation. This section is wet in places. Drop down and cross a wooden bridge with a handrail on the right. Continue along the path and over several short boardwalk bridges before descending steeply (beware of loose gravel) down to a broad forest track.

3. Turn right onto the track and follow it downhill towards the fantastic view of Ben Nevis!

   Fassfern is a working forest so watch out for vehicles on this track.

4. Follow the track past the forest buildings and a clump of Scot's pines on the right to return to the car park.

In the area
The Jacobite Steam Train runs from Fort William to Mallaig between May and October. Following the route of the Hogwarts Express it crosses the famous Glenfinnan Viaduct, and there's time to get out at Glenfinnan to visit the station and museum. Advance booking is essential.
www.westcoastrailways.co.uk/Jacobite_Home.cfm Tel: 0845 1284681

Walk 16: Neptune's Staircase Fort William

Take a leisurely stroll along the towpath of the Caledonian Canal from the sea at Loch Linnhe to the top of Neptune's Staircase, Britain's longest staircase lock, with a stunning view of Ben Nevis on a clear day.

This is an easy path along a smooth gravel towpath with a gentle incline along the staircase itself. There is an alternative start should you want a shorter walk. Not only that, but there are picnic sites, a playground, pub and café along the route. Water edges are unprotected so keep children under control.

Distance:	2.5 miles (4.5 km)
Allow:	1 hour 30 mins
Map:	Ordnance Survey 1:25 000 OL392
Grid reference:	098767

Getting there: Park at the quayside by the station in Corpach, signposted from the A830. For a shorter walk, park at Banavie by the Moorings Hotel, cross the canal by the lower lock and follow the instructions from 2.

From the car park, walk down the canal side towards the lighthouse. Go through the gap by the gate and turn left to cross the canal by the lock (Corpach Sea Lock). Turn left at the picnic site and walk along the towpath.

Though both towpaths are suitable for wheels, there is an unpleasant level crossing on the opposite side of the canal. Having experienced it solo with two children in tow, it is not recommended!

Follow the towpath past the houses ignoring minor paths down to the right.

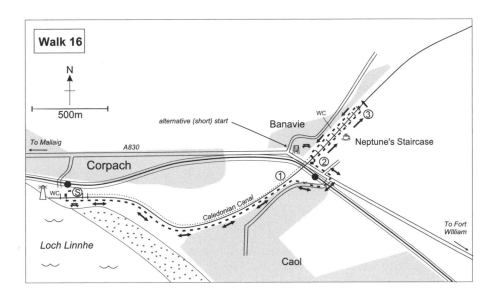

This is the Caledonian Canal, which runs for 62 miles SW-NE across Scotland from Corpach, near Fort William to Inverness. It takes advantage of the alignment of lochs along the Great Glen Fault and the canal was designed by Thomas Telford. It was built between 1803 and 1822 to join the lochs and to provide a route between the east and west coasts. In its time, it was the biggest waterway in Britain, even though the canal itself only occupies around a third of the total length. The Great Glen Fault is a major strike-slip fault (like the San Andreas), which brought rocks hundreds of miles from the NE. The rocks on the other side of the fault (roughly where you're parked) came from Norway!

1. Just before you reach the railway bridge, turn right down a path by a wooden post with a hexagon symbol. Join the road and turn left. Follow the road round to the level crossing (barrier) and cross carefully. Turn left onto the main road and walk past the station.

2. Cross the road carefully and go through the gate next to the small building to regain the canal towpath. You are now at Neptune's Staircase. **For a shorter walk, you can start from here.**

   This is the longest staircase lock in the UK comprising eight locks (16 gates), which lift boats a total height of 19.5 m. Designed by Thomas

Telford and built in the early 1800s, it takes boats 1.5 hours to get up the staircase! Originally hand-powered, the locks are now hydraulic and the traffic they carry is mostly pleasure boats.

Head along the towpath, now at a slight incline, past the staircase locks. You can get onto the locks and there is a great view up and down the staircase. Pass the café and teddy shop and continue to the last lock, beyond which is a basin with moored boats.

3. Cross by the top lock and return along the opposite towpath, past the handsome canal buildings. Walk back down the staircase and, at the bottom, you'll find a picnic area and playground in the car park next to a pub!

   When you've finished, cross by the lowest lock and return to the road. Cross the road and turn left to walk past the station. Turn right and head back down to the level crossing. Cross the railway

Neptune's Staircase on the Caledonian Canal

with care and fork right on the bend to rejoin the towpath. Follow the towpath all the way back to the sea locks and picnic site.

Here you get a great view of Ben Nevis, Britain's highest mountain at 1,344 m.

Cross the canal by the lower lock to return to your car.

In the area

Treasures of the Earth Centre, Corpach is just 4 miles from Fort William and has an outstanding collection of priceless gemstones, beautiful crystals (some weighing over 100 kg) and fossil remains from 500 million year old Trilobites to the skull of a sabre tooth tiger! Open all year round. Tel: 01397 772283

Walk 17: Glen Nevis, Fort William

☺ ◯ ⚲ 🥾 £ WC ☕ 🍺 ⛱

Glen Nevis is tucked away on the eastern side of Ben Nevis, Britain's highest mountain, and is a spectacular example of a glacial valley. It is a beautiful spot with lovely mountain views, and the River Nevis varying from calm and ponderous to a raging torrent, depending on the state of the weather.

This circular walk is a combination of waymarked routes and takes you up the riverside before returning through mixed woodland and past two cafés! The riverside path is narrow and rocky in places with some awkward tree roots, but the forest tracks are well maintained. Riversides are unprotected, so keep children under control, and the path can flood. If flooded, an alternative outward route is given.

Distance: 3.7 miles (6 km)
Allow: 2 hours
Map: Ordnance Survey 1:25 000 OL392
Grid reference: 121730

Getting there: Glen Nevis is signposted from the A82 north of Fort William. Park at the Visitor Centre (fee). The walk can also be started at the Braveheart car park.

From the Visitor Centre (toilets, shop, baby changing) follow the signposted 'Riverside Path' past the picnic tables. Walk along the gravel path to the suspension bridge (bouncy!) and cross the river. Go over the rocky patch and follow the path on the opposite side of the river, awkward in places with rocks and roots.

To start the walk from the Braveheart car park (yes it is named after the film – it was created to park the set lorries and caravans during filming), turn down the path by the disabled spaces to the bridge, follow the instructions from 5 to get to the Visitor Centre and continue as above.

Please note: The river does flood, so if it is high this section of

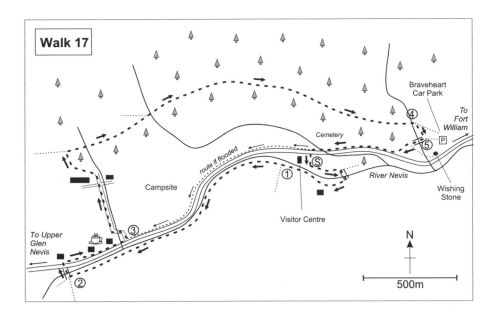

the walk will be impassable. Instead, return to the Visitor Centre
and walk up the road until you reach the Nevis Café. Turn right into
the café car park and follow the instructions from 3.

1. At the junction with the 'Ben Path', bear right to follow the river bank.

   Ahead you get lovely views up the glen to the pointed peak of Sgurr
   a'Mhaim and the lower slopes of Ben Nevis on your left.

   Continue past a wall on your right (muddy!), cross two narrow
   wooden bridges (wider pushchairs may need to wheelbarrow) and
   go up over awkward tree roots, after which the path gets easier.
   Carry on, crossing several more narrow bridges (wider pushchairs
   may need to remove a back wheel on the last) and turn right to
   cross the River Nevis via the large, grey bridge.

2. Cross the road opposite the Youth Hostel and turn right to walk
   along the pavement, past Café Beag and the Nevis Café and Bar.
   Turn left immediately after the Nevis Café.

Riverside rambling in Glen Nevis

3. Walk through the car park and up the road towards some black, wooden houses. Continue straight ahead at the cross-roads, past the houses and round to the left, where the road changes into a track at a gate. Go through the small gate on the right and head uphill on the good stony track into the trees. At the top of the hill turn right onto a broad forest track and continue gently uphill through mixed woodland.

   At the next junction continue straight ahead, signposted Braveheart Car Park. At the 'Peat Track' cross-roads, ignore a path on the right to the Visitor Centre and instead carry straight on past the log benches.

4. When you cross a stream (wooden handrail on the right) turn right down a narrow gravel path and past a picnic bench. This takes you down to a curved wooden bridge, turn right here and cross the bridge.

Alternatively, follow the track back to the Braveheart Car Park.

5. Continue straight ahead along the gravel path (left takes you on a detour to the Wishing Stone) and follow the path through young woodland with stunning views up the glen. When you reach the road, turn right and walk along the pavement to the Visitor Centre.

If you have time, it is well worth driving further up the valley, at least as far as the Lower Falls as the scenery is stunning.

In the area
Ben Nevis Gondola offers a fantastic opportunity to climb to a height of 650 m above sea level within 15 minutes of stepping onto the gondola! The journey affords spectacular views of the Scottish Highlands, including the Great Glen, Ben Nevis, and, on a clear day, the Inner Hebrides. Each gondola can hold up to 6 people and the operators are great at slowing down or stopping the gondolas to let you get everyone (plus pushchair) on board. Mountain trails to panoramic viewpoints, great sledging area (winter only), restaurant and bar are all easily accessed from the upper gondola station. Open all year round, with the exception of mid November to mid December for maintenance and windy days, which can restrict the operation of the gondolas. www.nevisrange.co.uk Tel: 01397 705825

Walk 18: Glencoe Lochan and Woodland, Glencoe

This walk combines two waymarked forest trails in the Glencoe Estate woodlands to give a varied route, with great views of lochans and mountains. The lochan and many of the paths were built by Lord Strathcona in the 19th Century and it is a beautiful place, with a wonderful view of the Pap of Glencoe across the lochan.

Though the full route is tough going in places, the short 1 mile route around the lochan is suitable for double off-roaders and buggy boards, and the path to access the lochan was built in gentle zig-zags (with rest benches) to make it suitable for wheelchairs. Good paths all the way, but the woodland section is very undulating with some short, steep ascents.

Distance: 1/2.5 miles (2/4 km)
Allow: 45 mins/1 hour 30 mins
Map: Ordnance Survey 1:25 000 OL384
Grid reference: 104594

Getting there: Turn off the A82 towards Glencoe Village/Kinlochleven. Turn immediately right signposted 'Museum, Hospital' to drive through the centre of the village and over the bridge. Turn left by the lodge, marked with a green Forestry Commission sign 'Glencoe Lochan'. Drive up the track, taking the right fork towards the lochan. Park in the car park at the end of the road.

he walk starts along the red route, so follow the red feather waymarkers up the easy access zig-zags to a cross-roads where you turn left. Climb up the gentle slope, ignoring paths to the left and right until you reach Glencoe Lochan by a green wooden hut.

Now owned by the Forestry Commission, the lochan and surrounding woodland were created in the 19th Century by Lord Strathcona on the Glencoe estate.

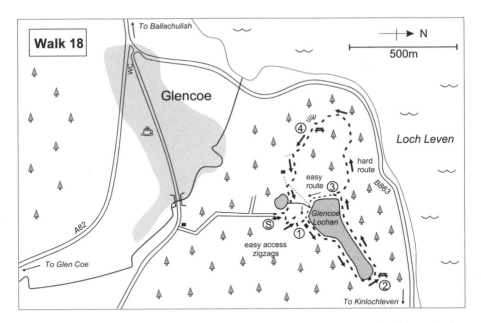

His wife was Canadian and of Native American heritage, and although the woodland was created to help her feel at home, she never settled.

1. At the hut, go straight ahead to walk around the lochan along the smooth, level gravel path (very easy going!).

   Look out for dense firs on your right and the small islands in the lochan, which are now covered in rhododendrons. It's also worth heading out onto the wooden platforms for the view over the water, but bear in mind they wobble as they are floating. There are also strategically placed benches and picnic tables along the way!

2. At the end of the lochan, you get a lovely view along its length to Creag Gorm on the other side of Glen Coe. Ignore the blue route to the right and bear left to walk back along the opposite shore.

   Watch out for a great view of the Pap of Glencoe (Sgorr na Ciche) which is reflected in the water on a clear day.

3. Pass two wooden platforms and continue to a picnic table, where you have two options:

For the easy route, stay on the main path and bear round to the left to cross the dam. Turn right by the green hut and simply follow the zig-zags back to the car park.

For the harder woodland route, turn right by the picnic table to follow the yellow markers into the woodland. This section of the route is rougher and quite steep in places.

Follow the obvious path passing tall Scot's pines, with undergrowth of rhododendrons, mosses and ferns. Follow the undulations, steep in places, out of the rhododendrons and into dense pine forest and then mixed woodland. Go uphill over a rough stretch taking care as there is a drop to the right.

As you head back down into pine forest, you get a view of Loch Leven through the trees to your right. Look out for the giant redwoods!

Continue along the path, which has some awkward tree roots, until it levels out temporarily at a viewpoint with a picnic table for a well deserved break!

Here you get a lovely view down Loch Leven towards Ballachulish with Creag Ghorm on the left and Beinn am Aonaich Mhoir on the right-hand shore. The viewpoint is fenced, but be aware of drops on either side and keep children under control.

4. Carry on along the undulating path from the viewpoint, rocky in places, to a fork where you take the left branch heading slightly uphill. Follow this path until you descend through the woods to a T-junction. Turn right and then immediately left, following the yellow arrows, to bump down some easy steps and join a second, lower track. Turn left and walk away from the house, following a flat path past a lily pond on your right until you reach the car park.

In the area

The Ice Factor, Kinlochleven is an award winning adventure centre on the west coast of Scotland. Indoor ice wall (five times bigger than any other in the world, teenagers and adults only though!) and rock climbing, tree top adventure course with tower, abseiling, giant swing, bike hire, shop, restaurant and a great indoor play area are available all year (7 days a week). www.ice-factor.co.uk Tel: 01855 831100

Admiring the Pap of Glencoe

Walk 19: Cruachan Reservoir, Loch Awe

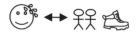

Ben Cruachan is Oban's local Munro. The reservoir, created on its slopes is man-made and was built between 1959 and 1965 to provide power for the world's first underground pump storage station. The reservoir service track provides an ideal route to take your pushchair into the heart of the Cruachan massif! Surrounded by beautiful mountain scenery, the reservoir is a tranquil place to sit and take in the scenery, views and, of course, eat your lunch!

This is a tough walk, despite being on metalled track to the dam, as the first 2¹/₂ miles are all uphill. At the end of the road, you can continue along the reservoir on a rough track. There are no obstacles, but we recommend two people to take turns to push as this walk is a real workout!

Distance:	6 miles (10 km)
Allow:	4 hours
Map:	Ordnance Survey 1:25 000 OL377
Grid reference:	114267

Getting there: Park in the village of Loch Awe on the A85 between Tyndrum and Oban, in the layby opposite St Conan's Kirk.

Walk along the pavement past St Conan's Kirk and turn right up St Conan's Road.

The kirk is worth a visit and was built between 1881 and 1931, with stone from boulders rolled from the nearby hillsides. The outside is lavishly decorated with almost every style of architectural embellishment! The interior is more subdued, with beautiful cloisters and chancel, and a life-like image of Robert the Bruce.

On the way back down from Cruachan Dam

Walk uphill past the houses and go through the gate onto the private road, which has an unusual speed limit!

1. As you walk up the road, you get great views down to Loch Awe to your left. Watch how the views change as you traverse the hillside.

   Pass a farm on your left, ignoring driveways and paths to your left. Cross the cattle grid and continue along the road, which is steep in places, and over several streams. As the road levels out, it bends to the right up the valley.

   From the bend, there is a great view down the Pass of Brander to Mull across the sea. Loch Awe drains through the pass and meets Loch Etive at Taynuilt. Legend says that a witch lived high on Cruachan and guarded a spring on the peak. She covered the spring at night and uncovered it again at sunrise, but one night she forgot and the spring overflowed. The water carved the Pass, flooded the land and the witch was turned to stone in punishment.

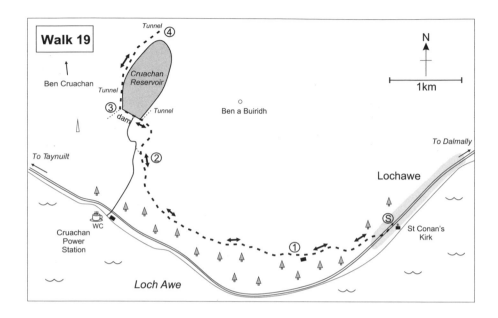

2. Continue up the valley amongst stunning mountain scenery and shortly the dam will come into view.

At the junction below the dam, continue straight ahead taking the right hand fork. Go steeply uphill (this is a slog!) to the dam. Go through the gate and turn left onto the dam.

If the power station is working, you can sit and watch the water levels go up and down as the water thunders down the pipes to the generators on the edge of Loch Awe.

3. Go through the gate on the far side of the dam and follow the track uphill as it zig-zags left and then right. The tarmac ends by a parking area.

At the fork, turn right and walk along the rough track by the reservoir. Pass a tunnel entrance.

The tunnels were built for capturing water higher on the hillside and channelling it into the reservoir.

4. The track goes to the end of the reservoir, so continue as far as you like – there are plenty of grassy areas to sit and enjoy the scenery. Return the way you came, taking care on the steep downhill sections (a leash is essential) and absorbing the views to the glen below.

In the Area

Cruachan 'The Hollow Mountain' is a great attraction on a wet day! It's hard to imagine from the outside, but the mountain of Ben Cruachan hides a massive cavern, high enough to house the Tower of London, containing enormous turbines which turn water into electricity. Regular tours (pre-booking essential) take you to see the massive cavern and electricity generators. Visitor centre, exhibition, café (overlooking Loch Awe), picnic area and gift shop open February to mid-December (9.30 am – 4.45 pm summer; winter times can vary). www.visitcruachan.co.uk Tel: 01866 822618

Walk 20: Avich Falls, Dalavich, Loch Awe

Dalavich nestles on the western shore of Loch Awe, Scotland's longest inland loch. Both shores are forested, mainly with plantations but there are pockets of native deciduous woodland, which is being regenerated in places.

This lovely walk takes you up the wooded gorge of the River Avich, which cascades down a series of rock steps between Loch Avich above and Loch Awe below. The walk is on good paths all the way, although rocky in places, and there are some steep inclines. Walking children need to be kept under control as river edges are generally unprotected, though there is fencing at points with particularly steep drops.

Distance: 1.5 miles (2.3 km)
Allow: 1 hour
Map: Ordnance Survey 1:25 000 OL360
Grid reference: 969138

Getting there: Drive along the western shore of Loch Awe, accessible from Taynuilt on the A85 and Kilmelford (via Loch Avich, narrow but lovely road) or just north of Kilmartin on the A813. Follow the signs to Dalavich. Park in the Barnaline car park. Picnic tables. Café, pub and shop in Dalavich.

From the car park, walk past picnic tables and information boards to take the broad forest track straight ahead, following the blue markers. Climb the track as it zig-zags uphill and pass a building on the left.

1. Just after the building, turn right down a woodland path with a sign to 'Avich Falls Walk'. Follow the path as it contours high above the river valley, with glimpses of the water down below you. Drop down slightly to reach the lowest waterfall.

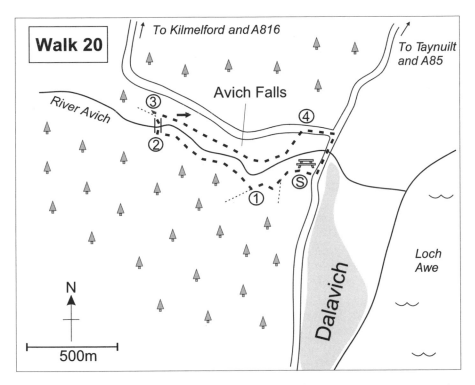

Walk 20

To Kilmelford and A816

To Taynuilt and A85

River Avich

Avich Falls

③ ② ④ ① Ⓢ

N

500m

Loch Awe

Dalavich

The river tumbles over a series of knobbly rocky steps. You can access the river at this point if little ones want to throw stones! Although the river is surrounded by pine plantation, the glen itself is wooded with ash, birch, lime and oak. Look out for wild flowers, ferns and mosses around the route.

Continue along the path as it climbs steeply above the waterfalls below you to the right and then undulates along the river side. Drop steeply down a rough section of path to reach a footbridge. A leash is advisable at this point.

2. Cross over the bridge and climb uphill beside fencing until you reach a T-junction with a forestry track.

Look out for bilberries which make a tasty snack in summer.

3. Turn right and walk along the track past the blue marker. Continue downhill, past tall pine trees until the falls become visible once more.

Take a short detour to the right, to reach a spectacular viewpoint with a bench to admire the falls in all their glory.

Return to the track, turning right to continue down the valley. The track turns away from the river and climbs slightly into the pine plantation. Carry on until you reach a gate, go round it to the right, and continue until you reach a T-junction with a road.

4. Turn right onto the road and follow it along, looking out for traffic. At the next T-junction, turn right towards Dalavich and walk along the road, crossing the river once more, until you reach the car park.

In the area

Loch Etive Cruises run 2 and 3 hour boat trips from Taynuilt up Loch Etive into the heart of the Glencoe Mountains that are inaccessible by road. Trips run from Kelly's Pier near Taynuilt village centre, March – December (Sunday – Friday). Tel: 01866 822 430

Avich Falls in spate

Walk 21: Inveraray Castle Woodland

Inveraray Castle is the family home of Lord Argyll, a member of the Campbell Clan who have lived on Loch Awe since around 1220, when they were placed in charge of the King's lands in this region. A stunning building dating from the 18th century, the castle is built from green rock and has four striking gothic turrets capped with conical roofs. It stands in a large estate with formal gardens, woodland, plantation and buildings. The woodland dates back to the 17th century when landowners were encouraged to plant trees.

This walk follows a waymarked trail around the lower wooded slopes of Dun na Cuaich – a prominent hill with a watch tower perched on top. The paths are good throughout, although there are some short steep inclines and the paths can be muddy in places. Dogs must be on a lead at all times and there is one kissing gate to lift the pushchair over.

Distance:	1.25 miles (1.5 km)
Allow:	1 hour
Map:	Ordnance Survey 1:25 000 OL360
Grid reference:	095092

Getting there: Park in either Inveraray or the castle car park. Access to the estate, shop and café is free.

From Inveraray, walk along the A83 in the Glasgow direction. Turn left along the castle drive and follow it all the way to the car park.

From the car park, head towards the castle entrance, and turn left following the waymarkers to the 'Woodland Walk' (yellow markers).

Carry on along the lane, passing a memorial urn on your left and crossing Frews bridge with its lovely stone balustrades.

The urn commemorates the execution of seventeen Campbell leaders in 1785 by the 1st Marquess of Atholl.

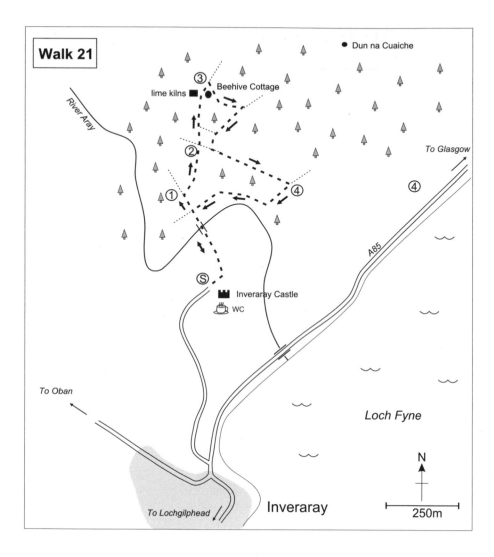

Continue along the lane, past a cross-roads until you reach a gravel lay-by.

1. Turn right here and head diagonally onto a woodland path marked by small blue and yellow arrows. Continue along the rough path which levels off, passing ruined buildings hidden amongst the trees.

This section can be muddy, but has lovely bluebells in spring.

Lift the pushchair over a kissing gate and go straight ahead across the track and follow a grassy path uphill towards a large gate leading into the woodland.

2. Join another track and turn left, through the gate following the arrows. Pass more ruined buildings on your left and continue until you reach a stand of Scot's pines with tall, straight trunks about 50 m after the buildings.

These buildings, with brick-edged arched windows were once lime kilns.

3. Turn right here to follow a path marked by yellow arrows. Pass a circular cottage with a collapsed roof and continue along the path, dropping downhill into dense fir trees.

This is Beehive or Limekiln Cottage, a listed building designed around 1800 by the architect Alexander Nasmyth. It was a round cottage suitable for a family, but a tree appears to have fallen on the building and badly damaged the roof.

Follow the path to a T-junction and turn right onto a track. Go through a gate and head downhill, bearing left at a junction and continue straight on. Drop down to a second track and turn left towards a gate marked with a yellow arrow. Go through the gate and walk along the track with woodland on your right and lovely views towards the Arrochar Alps ahead of you.

4. Go through a gate to a T-junction. Turn right and follow the track, which meets the river next to a twisted tree.

Through the trees you can see the castle on the other side of the river – the view is better in winter!

When you reach the lane, turn left and retrace your steps across Frew's bridge and back to the castle and car park.

Entrance to the café, shop and toilets are free, but there is a fee to visit the castle.

In the area

Inveraray Castle and Gaol – The castle dates from 1720 and is an imposing structure built from striking green stone. A tour of the castle reveals suits of shining armour, an impressive array of weaponry, ancient tapestries and an insight into the lives of the gentry past and present. In contrast, the Gaol housed men, women and children guilty of crimes from trespass to murder. Conditions were a stark contrast to those in the castle! Gaol open all year from 10 am, under 5s free (www.inverarayjail.co.uk Tel: 01499 302381). Castle open April – October from 10 am (www.inveraray-castle.com Tel: 01499 302203).

Helping Dad at Inveraray Castle

Walk 22: Ardkinglass Woodland Garden, Cairndow

 £ WC

Ardkinglass Woodland Garden, nestling in a valley on the shores of Loch Fyne, is an area of 25 acres of beautiful woodland. The planting, which began in the 1700s, led to the development of spectacular collections of rhododendrons and conifers, and the garden is home to some magnificent trees. As well as the plant collections, there are gazebos, poetry, beautiful lily ponds and the River Kinglass rushing through the bottom of the glen.

This route takes you round the main features of the garden and past some very tall trees! It is impossible to avoid all the steps, but the majority are downhill so it is not advisable to reverse the route. It should be noted that one flight leads to a steep river bank which is unprotected, though the path along the bank is good. There is one stream that requires you to lift the pushchair.

Distance: 1.25 miles (1.5km)
Allow: 1 hour
Map: Ordnance Survey 1:25 000 OL363
Grid reference: 179105

Getting there: Ardkinglass Woodland Garden is signposted from the A83 between Glasgow and Inveraray at Cairndow. Park in the car park. There is an entry fee to access the garden. Picnic tables and a portaloo are next to the car park.

From the car park, pass the kiosk and then follow the path straight ahead and up some easy shallow steps. Cross two wooden bridges and up four more steps (you can wheelbarrow to the right of these).

Look out for the Gunnera (giant rhubarb!) in the glen below.

Continue along the path and wheelbarrow past a flight of four more steps.

1. At marker post 4, take a detour left, reverse or carry the pushchair up four steps and visit the gazebo.

The gazebo provides benches and shelter – the garden has a high annual rainfall, which helps it flourish! Wooden plaques around the walls of the gazebo are carved with lines of poetry and prose.

Return to the main path and continue along, ignoring steps to your left. At the triangular junction bear left following the signpost to the Lochan and Old Mill.

Below you is Bodnant bank, home to the garden's rhododendron collection, many of which were transported to the garden by train from Bodnant Gardens in North Wales.

At marker post 6, go over a wooden bridge to cross the lochan which is covered in water lilies.

The lochan was made and planted in 2001/2002 to enhance the environment for woodland wildlife. In spring, this area is carpeted with bluebells. There is a viewing platform out over the water but beware this is unfenced!

2. At the steps turn right, put the pushchair on a leash and head downhill, bumping down two sets of three steps and then a steep flight of steps leading to the river bank. **Please note: The river bank is unprotected and there is a steep drop to one side so keep children and pushchairs under strict control!**

There are windows cut in the tree canopy for you to see the River Kinglass rushing through the glen below you. Look out for water birds including dippers and wagtails.

Continue along the path high above the river. The path is rocky in places and you need to look out for tree roots. Lift the pushchair over a little rocky stream, after which the path gets easier as you pass into pine woodland.

Look out for bracket fungi on dead tree trunks. The weir below you in the river was built to supply the house with hydro-electricity.

3. At the junction, go left and join the road next to a bridge. Turn right and walk along the road, away from the bridge, until you reach a black metal gate with a green sign. Go through the gate to re-enter the garden by the 'Tallest Tree', which is huge!

The tree, a grand fir, was planted in 1875 and was the tallest tree of any species in Britain for 10 years, reaching a maximum height of 208ft . Dieback at the growing tip lost it the title, although it is still one of the tallest grand firs in Britain. The tallest tree, at time of writing, was a Douglas fir found at nearby Dunans Castle, south of Strachur.

Bear left towards the tree following the green arrow. Pass a monkey puzzle tree and continue to the 'Mightiest Conifer' with its multitude of trunks.

This is a European silver fir and is thought to be over 250 years old - the oldest tree in the garden. Its unusual shape is thought to have developed

early in its growth due
to either poor manage-
ment or damage. In
1905 it measured
144ft and was last
measured at 169ft – a
truly mighty tree!

4. Continue along the
   lower path, past
   cedars, redwoods,
   hemlocks and
   rhododendrons.
   Follow the path
   round to the right
   and at the junction
   bear left following
   the signpost to the
   car park avoiding
   any steps. Cross
   over a wooden
   bridge and continue
   along the path, past
   marker post 12 all
   the way back to the
   car park and picnic
   area.

Big trees at Ardkinglass

In the area

Strachur Smiddy is a mini-museum in the centre of the village of Strachur off the A815. A reconstruction of the old village smiddy, it is full of tools of the trade, with the anvil standing proud in the middle of the room. You can try to use the bellows, test the ring of the anvil and find out about the craft of the blacksmith. Open daily, Easter – September, 1–4 pm (Tel: 01369 860508). For food, the tea room at the post office on the A886 Colintrave Road does good home-cooked food and caters for little ones. Also includes baby changing facilities.

Walk 23: Ardgartan Woodland, Arrochar

Ardgartan Forest is located on the shores of Loch Long close to the town of Arrochar, in a steep sided valley amongst the mountains known as the Arrochar Alps. The woodland is a mixture of deciduous forest and coniferous plantation and is home to the tumbling Croe Water river.

This walk is a combination of waymarked routes taking in wooded riverside, pebbly shore (with stunning views!) and plantation. The paths are narrow and rough in places and there is one short, but very steep ascent for which we recommend two people.

Distance:	2 miles (3 km)
Allow:	1 hour 30 mins
Map:	Ordnance Survey 1:25 000 OL364
Grid reference:	269037

Getting there: The Ardgartan Visitor Centre is on the A83 between Arrochar and Inveraray. Toilets, snacks, ice creams, information and maps available.

From the car park, go past the otter carving and through the picnic site to follow a good gravel path into woodland next to the river. Watch out for cyclists where advised. At the fork in the path bear right and stay close to the river. Pass a wall, negotiate the tree roots and continue alongside the river, which is full of giant boulders. The path is narrow in places with more roots and a couple of boulders to negotiate.

At a red marker by a bank, stay down by the river and follow it around the bend until you have to turn up a path, which leads up the bank (this route is easier for a pushchair than the way-marked steps!). Rejoin the main gravel path and continue along the path by the river.

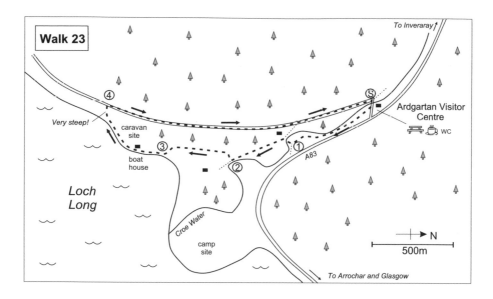

1. At the next junction, turn right to walk over the bridge. Join the track and turn left, through the gatehouse and past the pink Ardgartan Lodge. Continue down the track above the river.

2. Pass a ruined cottage and turn right just before a driveway to follow the blue marker along a field path towards the loch shore.

   This stretch of path has great views across Loch Long and the carpets of bluebells in spring are stunning.

   Continue along the path, rocky in places and head downhill into the woods. Negotiate a rocky step and cross a wooden bridge, which has a step on the far side. Go through a field and follow a little stream down to the pebbly loch shore.

3. At the shore, turn right to follow the path above the beach.

   This is a great spot for a break, some stone skimming and a paddle.

   The path drops down to meet the shore at the boat house. Go up a steep rock step and continue along the path past the caravan site, ignoring the gate into the site. Pass a stile on the right, cross

Tumbling Croe Water

a small stream and go up the steep rocky slope to the fencing at the road. **Though only short, this slope is a tough push and the path surface isn't great. Two people are recommended.**

4. Join the road and turn right. Follow the road uphill and walk along with plantation forest on the left. Head along the road until you reach the bridge. Turn right and cross the bridge to return to the Visitor Centre and your car.

In the area

Loch Lomond Aquarium is a sea life conservation and rescue centre which makes a great day out. Rockpools, ray tanks, sharks and otters sit alongside waterfalls and a deep loch. With a cinema, café and regular events throughout the day there is plenty to entertain everyone. Located at Loch Lomond Shores off the A82 - follow signs for Balloch and Loch Lomond Shores. Open daily from 10am, except Christmas Day. www.sealife.co.uk Tel: 0871 4232110

Walk 24: Kilmun Arboretum, Dunoon

Kilmun Arboretum is a hidden gem in the forests that cloak the hills across the waters of the Holy Loch from Dunoon. It was established in the 1930s as a test area to see which trees would thrive in this coastal climate. It is home to a wonderful collection of 260 tree species from all around the world, many of which are now endangered in their native environments. Unlike many arboreta of Victorian collectors, which typically just have one individual of each type of tree, Kilmun is special in that each plot is like a mini-woodland of a particular tree type, which enables you to really appreciate their beauty in numbers.

This walk is a combination of waymarked routes through the arboretum and, although short, it is a strenuous walk with some steep inclines both up and downhill. There are unprotected drops around the walk and a pushchair leash is essential, especially for the descents. Particular care also needs to be taken of walking children. There are a couple of opt-out shortcuts on this route – just follow the alternative directions given if you don't want to do the whole walk!

Distance:	1 mile (1.6 km)
Allow:	1 hour
Map:	Ordnance Survey 1:25 000 OL363
Grid reference:	164821

Getting there: Follow the A880 along the northern shore of Holy Loch towards Strone. The arboretum is poorly signposted in the village of Kilmun – the sign is actually at the junction, but if you miss it you can turn round in the lay-by in front of the church. Turn up the steep track and park in the car park on the left where there are information boards.

From the car park, take the lower path marked with red and yellow markers – this route initially follows the red route.

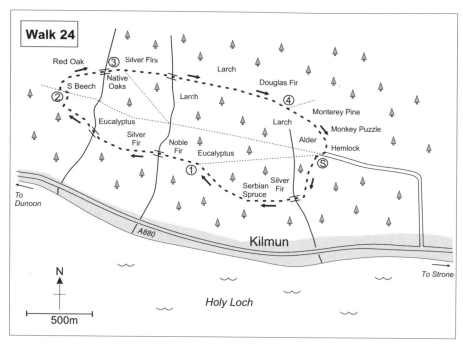

Look out for the small, green information boards as you walk around the route. These tell you what trees are in each plot, where they originate and any special features. In addition, there are swing-out signs with more general information.

Descend steeply through Tulip Trees and Sitka Spruces and follow the path round to the right into the European Silver Fir plot. Go over a bridge, past a group of Cypresses and into Serbian Spruce, which are endangered in the wild. Pass a bronze-leaved Maple and start to head uphill.

1. The path levels out at a junction where you turn left.

    Right takes you back to the car park along the yellow route. There is a bench here and if you stop for a rest, breathe deeply to smell the Eucalyptus trees surrounding you!

    Head uphill through Eucalyptus, Noble Fir and Cypresses and cross a bridge over a small stream. **There is a steep drop to the left here,**

so put the pushchair on a leash. Continue uphill through more firs and then Peppermint Trees – a form of Eucalyptus, and head round to the right.

The number and variety of Eucalyptus trees is a special feature of the arboretum.

The path levels out as you head past a bench and then over another small stream. Head uphill again, which gets very steep for the last push up to a T-junction with a broad forestry track.

2. Turn left and then immediately right to continue further uphill, still following the red markers.

If you have had enough climbing (though the worst is over!), just turn right along the forestry track which will take you back to the car park – recommended if you don't like steep descents.

As you climb uphill you pass through Southern Beech and Red Oaks (lovely leaf colours in autumn), and British native Oaks on the right. Continue through Birches and Beeches as the path levels off and walk through a patch of Silver Firs.

3. At the next junction, leave the red route and carry on straight ahead contouring along the hillside.

Following the red markers downhill takes you back to the forestry track, where you turn left to return to the car park.

Go through Sakhalin Firs and continue along the path, heading down to a bridge over a cascading stream.

Eventually, through the trees, you see a view of Holy Loch below you with Dunoon on the opposite shore.

Pass a bench and continue along the path past Larch trees. **There is a steep drop to your right here and a short fence guards a hole in the ground.**

4. At the next junction, take the fork right to follow the blue route,

Resting in a Eucalyptus grove, Kilmun Arboretum (not Australia!)

which takes you downhill through Monterey Pines and then a Monkey Puzzle forest on your left! **Please note: This descent is steep! A leash is essential.**

Pass more Larch trees on your right and then just as the view opens out below you, there are Western Hemlock on the left with Alder on the right. Continue to the track where you turn left to end your tour of the world's trees and return to your car.

There are facilities in Kilmun and at the head of Holy Loch.

In the area
Riverside Swim Centre, Dunoon has a full sized and toddler pool with a 40m flume you can see as you drive along the sea front! For grown ups there is a sauna, steamroom, spa, relaxation area and gym. There is also a café serving healthy food. Open daily, phone 01369 701170 for pool times and prices.

Walk 25: Bishop's Glen, Dunoon

Bishop's Glen is a hidden valley up above Dunoon. It houses a reservoir that once supplied the town with drinking water, but is now purely recreational, although the dam and weir are still intact. Surrounded by both native woodland and coniferous plantation, the lake is a good place for spotting wildlife, in particular red squirrels, woodpeckers, dragonflies and herons.

This walk takes you around the resevoir and then out into woodland before returning along a stream to a lovely picnic area. Paths are good all the way round, but there are two flights of steps heading downhill. The walk cannot be reversed due to the steps.

Distance: 1.5 miles (2.5 km)
Allow: 1 hour 15 minutes
Map: Ordnance Survey 1:25 000 OL363
Grid reference: 165766

Getting there: From the seafront and ferry terminal, head south past a café and crazy golf course. Follow the road as it curves round to the right (Tom-a-Mhoid Road) and turn onto Achamore Road. Continue straight ahead when the road bends left. Turn right onto Alexander Street and then left up Nelson Street. Park in the car park at the top of Nelson Street or, if full, on the road.

From the car park, head straight ahead uphill along the metalled lane looking out for cars heading for the disabled car park (key available at the Tourist Information Centre for disabled visitors to park here). As you climb gradually uphill, pass a pond on the right and then a viewpoint on the left overlooking the Bradaigh Burn and the overflow weir for the dam below you.

1. When you reach the dam, just after a house, turn left and head along a gravel path below the dam and cross the bridge over the

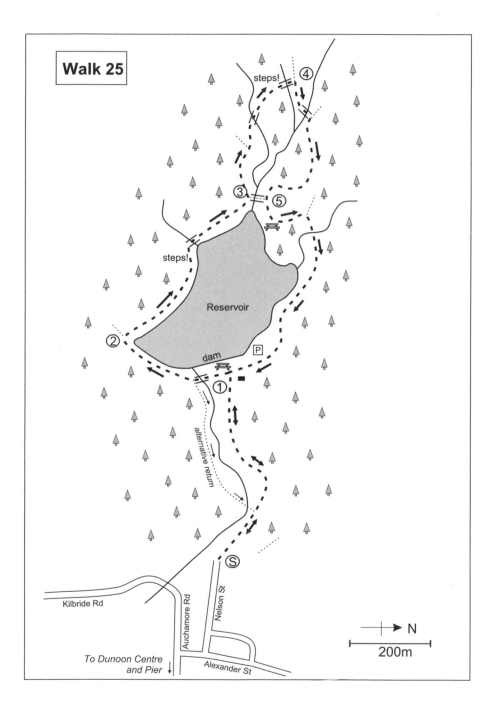

Walk 25

steps!
④
③
⑤
Reservoir
steps!
②
dam
P
①
alternative return
Ⓢ

Kilbride Rd
Auchamore Rd
Nelson St
Alexander St
To Dunoon Centre and Pier ↓

N
200m

outflow weir. Turn right on the other side of the bridge and head uphill along a rough section of gravel path. The path levels off just after a dam and you walk through mixed woodland.

There are good views of the resevoir to your right just after the dam wall. Look out for waterbirds and red squirrels.

A dreech day in Bishop's Glen!

2. Cross a small stream and pass a kissing gate on the left. Keep following the main path as it bends round to the right following the end of the resevoir. Bump down 13 steps (unlucky!) and cross a bridge over a stream. Follow the path through young birch trees with abundant ferns.

You can access a gravel beach on this stretch, but will have to park the pushchair. This is a popular spot for fishermen and also small children throwing stones...

3. Just before the next bridge, fork left to follow a path away from the resevoir into woodland with the stream on your right.

If you don't want to do this section, just cross the bridge and keep following the main path round the resevoir, rejoining the walk at number 5.

The path heads uphill and then levels off as you walk through the trees. Head downhill and bump down 14 steps to another wooden bridge over a stream. Push back up the other side after the bridge and follow the path through the woodland.

4. At the next T-junction, turn right to follow a path as it meanders through the trees by a stream towards a wooden footbridge. Cross this bridge and bear right past a bench. Continue until you reach the bridge you saw earlier at 3 and bear left to rejoin the shore.

5. Go past a lovely picnic area on the shore of the resevoir, following the path round to the left into tall fir trees and then right, ignoring a smaller path to the left. Continue past the barrier and through the disabled car park to rejoin the metalled road you walked up at the start of the route.

The section from the barrier to the picnic area is suitable for wheelchairs.

Follow the road past the dam and head left downhill.

Look out for the sculptures in the garden on the left!

Continue down the road and back to the car park at the bottom of the hill.

In the area

Castle House Museum, Dunoon is located in the former holiday home (or 'castle') of Lord Provost Ewing of Glasgow, which was built on the site of the town's original Mediaeval castle. It now houses a selection of exhibits telling the history of Cowal from the Stone Age to when it provided accommodation for an American naval base, including their nuclear submarines! It is set in lovely gardens with picnic areas, tennis courts and a putting green. Located opposite Dunoon Pier and the ferry terminal. Open Easter – October 10.30 – 4.30, accompanied children free. www.castlehousemuseum.org.uk Tel: 01369 701422

Walk 26: The Mull of Kintyre

The Mull of Kintyre sits at the southern end of the Kintyre Peninsula, which dangles down off the west coast of Scotland into the Irish Sea. The headland has extremely strong currents and is prone to mists, which may well have provoked the famous song... The Mull itself is a treeless rocky headland (Mull comes from the gaelic 'maol' meaning 'bald'), with precipitous cliffs and the lighthouse we're visiting on its western coast.

This is a steep walk, taking you down the access road to the lighthouse located on the cliffs below. The views are spectacular; across to Ireland only 12 miles away, and over to the islands of Islay, Jura and Gigha off the Kintyre coast. A leash on the pushchair is essential as the descent is steep, and we recommend 2 people for the walk back up the hill.

Distance:	2 miles (3 km)
Allow:	2 hours
Map:	Ordnance Survey 1:25 000 OL356
Grid reference:	597081

Getting there: Follow the signs from Campbeltown to Southend (great beach) and follow the road all the way to the end, signposted 'Mull of Kintyre Lighthouse'. Park in the layby, keeping the turning area clear. From the car park, head towards the gate and follow the path round it to the right. **Put the pushchair on a leash now!**

Follow the road as it zig-zags down the hill – there are crash barriers on the steepest sections.

Ahead of you is the northern tip of Ireland, with Rathlin Island just offshore. You may see its lighthouse flashing across the water.

As you come to the first crash barrier you can see the lighthouse below you. The gradient eases as you go under the telegraph wires

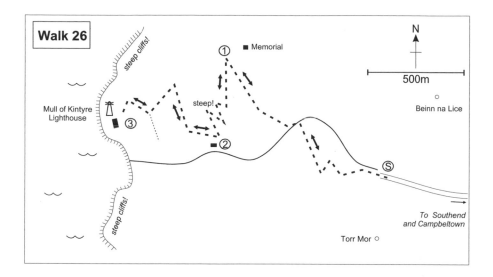

and you continue across the moorland, which turns purple with the flowering heather in late summer. Continue to the headland where the Paps of Jura come in to view.

Keep going downhill towards the sharp left hand bend and crash barrier.

To distract whisky drinkers from the steep slope, the two white buildings that can be seen on Islay are the distilleries of Laphroaig and Lagavulin!

1. Head round the sharp bend – this is the steepest section of the walk so take care!

   If you can't face the full descent we recommend turning back here. There is a great view below to the lighthouse and the old keepers' cottages (now holiday cottages). The keepers had a tough life, but were given extra salary to keep a horse, as one was needed to carry the stores from the storeroom 7 miles away!

2. Continue downhill round the sharp hairpins, past an old cottage on the left and all the way to the lighthouse.

   The lighthouse stands 240ft above the sea on a sheer cliff and was built in 1788 by Thomas Smith. It was one of the first to be built by the

Mull of Kintyre – without the mist rolling in from the sea…

Commissioners of Northern Lighthouses (now the Northern Lighthouse Board). The lighthouse was automated in 1996 and you get a good view of the lens in the light chamber, now powered by a 250W vapour lamp. Its signal is 2 white flashes every 20 seconds and it has a range of 24 miles.

3. Just past the cottages is a grassy area where you can rest before heading all the way back up the hill you just came down!

    If you complete the walk without having that song going round in your head you've definitely earned a whisky!

In the area

The Scottish Owl Centre, Campbeltown is home to Scotland's largest collection of owls, including both native and international species. Meet the owls, get the chance to hold one of these beautiful birds or watch the daily flying display. There is also an outdoor play area and tea room. Suitable for all ages and under-3s are free. Open 1.30 – 4.30 pm on Wednesday to Saturday, April-September. (Also open Monday and Tuesday in July and August). www.scottishowlcentre.com Tel: 01586 554397

Walk 27: The Goudrons, Machrihanish

Machrihanish, now famous for its Championship Links golf course, was once the site of coal mining and salt extraction from sea water! It was linked by narrow gauge railway to Campbeltown, which originally served the mines, but was extended to carry passengers with the onset of tourism. The area also has the largest dune system in Kintyre, designated as a conservation area, and is home to rare pyramidal and marsh orchids.

This is a short walk to the Galdrings, or Goudrons, a lovely and popular bay with stunning sea views. Going is good, but rocky in places and grassy paths can be indistinct. Suitable for double off-roaders.

Distance:	2 miles (3 km)
Allow:	1 hour
Map:	Ordnance Survey 1:25 000 OL356
Grid reference:	637207

Getting there: Machrihanish is signposted from Campbeltown at the end of the Mull of Kintyre. Park in the village opposite The Old Clubhouse pub.

Walk along the road to the end of the village, with the sea and beaches on your right.

There are lovely views across the sea to the islands of Gigha, Jura, with its twin Paps, and Islay to the left.

At the end of the houses continue, straight ahead along a single track road following it round to the left.

Look out for Eider ducks and seals in the water.

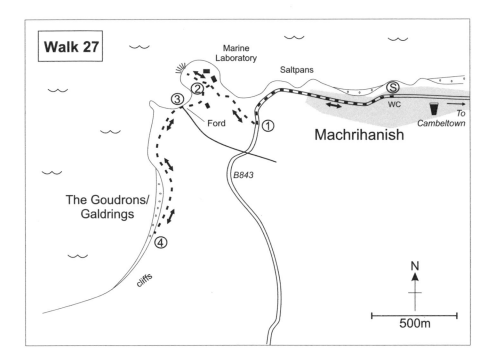

1. Turn right down a track in front of a low, white house with a sign saying 'Seabird Observatory, Beware of the Bull and 'The Galdrings'. Continue along the track and past the strange looking buildings (Stirling University's marine research station).

2. At the junction by the silos, carry on straight ahead to the viewpoint.

   There is a bird hide here and it has fantastic views across to Islay and Jura. The observatory is one of the top places in the area for watching sea birds.

   Head back to the track and take the left hand track heading slightly inland and across the grass.

3. Ford a stream and continue along the track. Ahead of you the cliffs of the Mull of Kintyre can be seen on a clear day (try not to sing...). Continue past some concrete ruins.

Off to paddle at the Galdrings

This was the site of a radio mast used to send the first wireless transmission across the Atlantic, which was made by the Canadian Reginald Fessenden in 1906. This site was chosen as it was believed that radio waves could not travel through or around hills and this spot gave a clear view across the Atlantic to the main transmission station at Brant Rock, Massachussets. The mast was 450 ft high and was tethered to the ground at the anchor points, which can still be seen around the base. Although there were early transmissions here, the site was short lived as storms broke the tethers and the mast buckled and collapsed in December 2006, ending Machrihanish's role in trans-Atlantic communications.

4. The track peters out, but continue across the slightly rocky grass which is good going. Carry on straight ahead until you reach the beach. Park the pushchair and go for a paddle!

Once you've finished, simply return the same way back to the village and your car, calling at one of the sandy beaches on the way. Machrihanish has a slightly less salubrious claim to fame in St Kevin. He inaugurated a custom where unhappily married couples gathered together in darkness and ran blindfolded three times around the chapel. On stopping, they would grab the nearest partner of the opposite sex who they were then married to for the next 12 months!

In the Area

Aqualibrium, Campbeltown is a state of the art building, which houses the library and swimming pool, providing a multi-functional leisure complex. Opened in 2006, there is the pool, gym, relaxation room, crèche and bistro. Located on Kinloch Green, just behind the Esplanade. Tel: 01586 551212 for opening times and prices.

Walk 28: Arichonan Township, Tayvallich

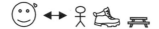

Arichonan sits high on the hills of northern Knapdale, overlooking Caol Scotnish and Loch Sween. Once a thriving community, Arichonan was deserted during the Highland Clearances, but its inhabitants didn't leave quietly! You can still see bedsteads and cauldrons in the houses, which offer plenty of opportunities for exploration.

A short, but initially steep walk through the forest brings you out in the ruined village with its spectacular views down the coast. The paths are rocky forest tracks and mown grass paths, and the going is good once the initial climb is over. Be aware of the dangers of potential falling masonry around the ruined buildings.

Distance: 1.5 miles (2 km)
Allow: 1 hour
Map: Ordnance Survey 1:25 000 OL358
Grid reference: 777910

Getting there: Park at the Gleann a Gealbhan car park located on the B8025 between Crinan and Tayvallich. Picnic tables located here.

Head up the car park entry road to the B8025.

1. Cross the road and join a small grassy path straight ahead, which turns immediately right to climb through the trees above and parallel to the road.

   Climb up the hill, over a couple of awkward tree roots and continue along the path, steep in places, until you reach the power lines at a T-junction.

2. Turn left here and continue uphill, more gently now, past coniferous plantation and along a mown grassy path. Follow the

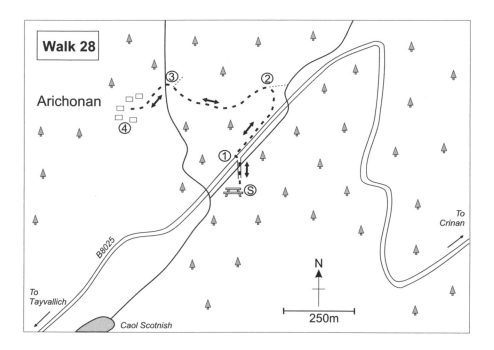

Walk 28

Arichonan

B8025

To
Tayvallich

Caol Scotnish

To
Crinan

N

250m

path beside the power lines onto more open hillside. Negotiate a couple of drainage ditches and some tree roots, and contour around the hillside above a farm.

From here, you start to get great views to the left down towards the inlet of Caol Scotnish and Knapdale.

3. Ignore steps to your right and cross a small stream via a bridge and keep going until you reach the ruined village of Arichonan. **Warning: these are ruined buildings and a sign warns you about falling masonry.**

Arichonan was the largest of five townships in the area stretching north towards Crinan. Inhabited since the 1600s, the village, which originally belonged to the McNeills and Campbells, ended up as part of the Poltalloch estate (the ruined manor house is south of Kilmartin). The tenants were served a Summons of Removing in spring 1848, stating that they, their families and chattels were to leave their homes by Whitsun. But in this village the residents did not want to leave! When the local Sheriff and

Exploring the ruins in Arichonan township

his men arrived to enforce the summons, they were met by a crowd of around 100 villagers and were attacked in an infamous riot! Several of the villagers spent time in Inveraray Jail … and all because the landowners discovered sheep made more money than the tenants. The buildings you see today date from this time – look for dates on the houses, thatch pegs and slots for roof crucks.

4.
Once you've finished exploring (and it is a great place for a picnic!!) simply retrace your route back to the car park.

In the area
Coffee Shop, Crinan Canal is a lovely tea room with delicious cakes, located at the western end of the 9 mile canal that cuts across the top of the Kintyre Peninsula. There are views of the boats as they pass through the locks, either into the canal or out into Loch Crinan. After you've eaten, there's plenty to explore in the canal basin, including a

stripy lighthouse and an old steam boat Puffer. You can also cross the lock gates, watch the sea locks fill (and empty!) with water and there's a towpath with spectacular views if you need to walk off the cakes.

Walk 29: Kilmartin Glen Archaeology Trail

Kilmartin is one of the most important archaeological sites in Europe and has been the site of human occupation since the first farmers settled here some 8000 years ago. There are 350 ancient monuments within 6 miles of the village, including some outstanding examples of prehistoric monuments.

This is an easy walk around some of the most important monuments near the village and it has some wonderful views. The glen was once the drainage route for Loch Awe before the effects of glaciation changed the path of the water to the north. Apart from the incline down from the village, the walk is level and the path is suitable for double pushchairs and strollers.

Distance:	2.5 miles (4 km)
Allow:	1 hour 30 mins
Map:	Ordnance Survey 1:25 000 OL358
Grid reference:	835988

Getting there: Kilmartin is located on the A816 between Oban and Lochgilphead. Park in the car park opposite the pub next to the church.

From the car park, walk towards the church and go through the gate into the churchyard.

Follow the path to the left of the church heading towards a glass roofed building. Go into the building on the far side of the churchyard to view the carved tombstones.

These stones were grave coverings which were originally laid flat in the churchyard. They were carved by local sculptors, whose work can be found throughout the area, and date from the 12th to 18th Centuries. Carvings

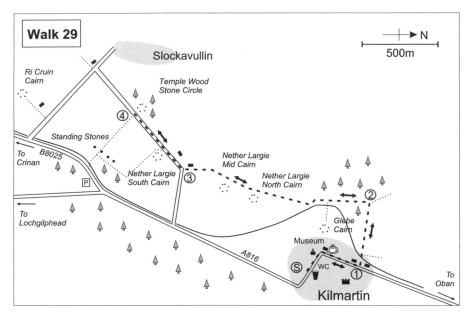

include armoured figures, celtic knotwork and grotesque animals. More carved stones can be found in the Poltalloch enclosure on the right towards the gate and carved crosses can be seen in the church.

Leave the building and head towards a black door in the wall with a sign 'Kilmartin House Museum'. Go through the door and into the museum area.

The museum has an entry charge, but you can find out more about the history of the glen and tickets are valid all day. Toilets (including disabled) and an excellent café.

Return to the road and turn left. Follow the pavement downhill through the village, looking out for Kilmartin Castle up to your right.

This is a fortified tower house dating from the 16th Century. It was restored in the 1990s and is now a private house.

1. Just after the garage, turn left down a track between two houses. Go over the river, across a cattle grid and continue straight ahead,

Snuggling up in the double buggy at Kilmartin

ignoring a track on your right. Look out for the large pile of stones in the field to your left; Glebe Cairn.

The cairn is over 33m across and concentric stone circles were found inside along with two human burials.

2. When the track bends round to the right, fork left along a level path with a smooth gravel surface. The start of this path can be muddy in wet weather.
    Continue along the path next to the river and through a gate. Pass the bridge, which is the path to Glebe Cairn. Though you can't get a pushchair to the cairn itself, you get a good view of the cairn from here and the bridge is good for Pooh-sticks!
    Just after the bridge, Nether Largie North Cairn comes into view.

This cairn is worth a visit as you can climb inside to see an important carved grave slab, with over 40 cup marks and some 10 axe heads carved into it. The quantity of carvings suggests this was the burial place of a

Stone Age VIP! You'll need to leave the pushchair with a responsible person though, as there is a low step stile to access the cairn.

Continue down the path to Nether Largie Mid Cairn.

Dating back about 4000 years, the cairn contained two burial cists, both empty at excavation. From here you get a good view of what was a linear cemetery, with the three Nether Largie Cairns, Glebe Cairn to the north and Ri Cruin Cairn to the south all in alignment.

3. Continue along the track until you reach the school on your right. Join the road and go straight ahead past Nether Largie house to Nether Largie South Cairn on the left.

This is the oldest cairn in the glen and is thought to be over 5000 years old! It was a chambered cairn, typical of those in this area, and the central chamber is open so you can see its structure.

Carry on down the road looking over the wall to your left. In the field is a large collection of standing stones, some in alignment and reaching several metres high.
Continue to Temple Wood, which is the last location on our walk.

Temple Wood contains two stone circles. The northern circle, closest to the gate, comprises a ring of rounded river stones with a central standing stone. There was originally a ring of posts, which is marked on the ground by concrete blocks in amongst the stones. The furthest, southern circle has 13 standing stones (although there may have been more originally) with a central stone burial cist surrounded by a circle of smaller stones, dating back 5000 years. This was also the site of several later burials, one containing a beaker, a habit well known elsewhere in Britain and leading to the name 'Beaker People'. The trees were planted in the 19th century to provide more atmosphere, when the name was also given. This is a lovely place to take a break and you can get the pushchair into the wood and right up to the stone circles.

4. Once you have finished at Temple Wood, retrace your steps back to the village to visit the museum and café or pub (both have highchairs and do excellent food).

In the area:

Carnassarie Castle is a 16th Century tower house and hall makes a perfect end to a day in Kilmartin Glen. Accessible by pushchair, except the few steps to reach the castle itself; you can carry the pushchair up the steps or take the baby out and leave the pushchair by the gate. Entry is free and there is an enclosed lawned area for the kids to have a run around. You can climb to the top of the towers, take in the view and explore the cellars. Unprotected drops and old masonry require you keep a close eye on children. Signposted off the A816 just north of Kilmartin village.

Walk 30: Bridgend Woodland, IIslay

Bridgend Woodland is one of several deciduous woods on Islay planted by the Victorian landowners. Now mature, the woodland is beautiful year round and in spring and summer is famed for its wild flowers and the sound of birdsong.

This route takes you on a circuit from Islay House Square, with its craft shops, café and brewery, through the woodland beside the River Sorn. Though the paths are well maintained, they are rough in places and stone slabs laid over wet areas may require wheelbarrowing.

Distance: 2.75 miles (4.5km)
Allow: 1 hour 30 mins
Map: Ordnance Survey 1:25 000 OL353
Grid reference: 339627

Getting there: From Bridgend, in the centre of the island, drive along the A846 towards Port Askaig and park in the car park on the left signposted 'Islay House Square'.

Go through the gate onto the drive, turn right, cross the road and head down the broad track opposite through a white gate signposted 'Bridgend Woods Path'. Follow the track through the woods to a T-junction.

1. At the junction turn left following the Bridgend Woods signpost.

    These are lovely deciduous woods with lush flower growth including snowdrops, daffodils, bluebells and comfrey, depending what time of year you visit.

    Continue along the path which joins and runs alongside the River Sorn. Keep going straight ahead ignoring a bridge and track to the

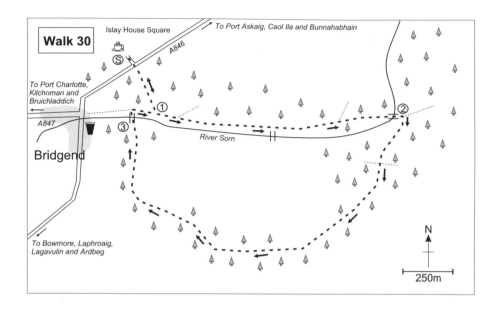

right. Go past a track to the left, continue to a bench and head towards a bridge where the river bends sharply to the left.

2. Cross the bridge and turn right, signposted 'Bridgend', to walk along a track through the trees. Continue along the track heading slightly uphill and through the woods. Go through a metal gate, cross the farm track and continue through the gate opposite into the woods.

   There are pink rhodedendrons in the woods, providing a riot of colour in spring.

   Pass a small stream and continue along the track which is quite rough in places, with an open field on your right. **The track can get wet, though there are slabs over the boggy stretches (you may need to wheelbarrow over some of these).**

   Continue along the path as it curves round to the right following the edge of the field until you come to a cross roads marked by two large tree stumps.

Bridge end at Bridgend…

3. Go between the stumps and continue straight ahead along a grassy path signposted 'Islay House'. Head across the wooden bridge (with a beautiful river view!) and turn right at the T-junction with a gravel track, signposted 'Islay House Square'.

   At the next junction turn left, to walk back along the track you started on, through the white gate and across the road to the car park.

In the area
Islay Distillery Tours: The small island of Islay has a grand total of nine whisky distilleries, each producing its own distinctive single malt; Caol Isla, Bowmore, Bunnahabhain, Bruichladich, Laphroaig, Lagavulin, Ardbeg, Port Charlotte and the recently opened Kilchoman. The distilleries offer tours where you can view the process from grain to barrel, including the malting process at Laphroaig, sample the product and maybe even invest in a barrel. Details of all the distilleries can be found at www.islayinfo.com or call tourist information in Bowmore Tel: 01496 810254.

More books for intrepid pushchair walkers!

ALL-TERRAIN PUSHCHAIR WALKS: SNOWDONIA

Zoë Sayer & Rebecca Terry

A superb collection of pushchair-friendly walks for North Wales. These 30 routes explore the spectacular scenery of the Snowdonia National Park – including an adventurous walk that takes you and a pushchair half-way up Snowdon! The walks range from simple riverside strolls to full-on alpine-style stomps.
£7.95

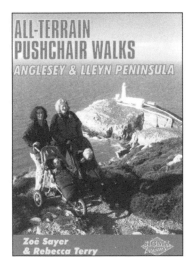

ALL-TERRAIN PUSHCHAIR WALKS: ANGLESEY & LLEYN PENINSULA

Zoë Sayer & Rebecca Terry

Pushchair walks by the sea — from beach strolls to cliff-top rambles. There are 30 tried-and-tested routes from simple beach strolls to rugged inland hill-top rambles through fields, woods and over hills and mountains with scarcely any obstacles and never any need to remove the child from the pushchair.
£7.95

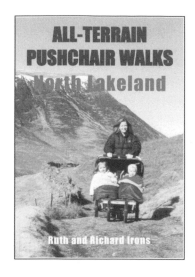

ALL-TERRAIN PUSHCHAIR WALKS: NORTH LAKELAND
Ruth & Richard Irons

Here are 30 walks across North Lakeland from Ennerdale Water to Lowther Park, Haweswater to Bassenthwaite. You'll find something to suit every type of walker – from Sunday Strollers to Peak Baggers and everyone else in between! Ruth and Richard Irons are experienced parents and qualified outdoor pursuits instructors – a reliable combination!
£7.95

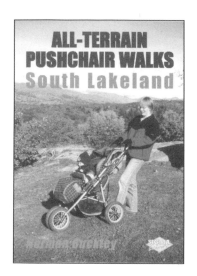

ALL-TERRAIN PUSHCHAIR WALKS: SOUTH LAKELAND
Norman Buckley

"This book is fantastic – a perfect guide for parents" – Kathleen Jones (Lakeland Book of The Year Awards, 2005). Enjoy fabulous Lakeland scenery – north to south, from Grasmere to Grizedale Forest, and west to east, from Coniston to Kendal – you'll be spoilt for choice!
£7.95

ALL-TERRAIN PUSHCHAIR WALKS: PEAK DISTRICT
Alison Southern
Level routes around Peak District villages and more adventurous (but safe) hikes across the moors. Alison is a parent of a young child and has an excellent knowledge of the Peak District. So now there's no reason to stay at home – here is the ideal opportunity to introduce the youngest children to the wide-open spaces of the Peak District!
£7.95

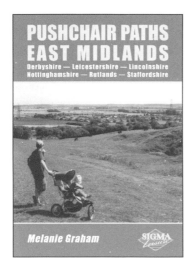

PUSHCHAIR PATHS: EAST MIDLANDS
Melanie Ramet
This is the first pushchair-friendly walking book for the East Midlands written by enthusiastic walker, writer and 'East Midlander', Melanie Ramet. Melanie has written 25 'ORPing' (Off-Road Pushchairing) routes to encourage unrestricted access into the heart of the wonderful East Midlands countryside, where walkers can be confident there will be no unexpected obstacles to negotiate the pushchair over, under or through!
£7.95

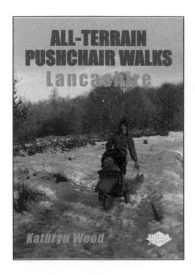

ALL-TERRAIN PUSHCHAIR WALKS: LANCASHIRE
Kathryn Wood

The 10th in the highly successful 'All-Terrain Pushchair Walks' series. 30 Graded walks around the county of Lancashire, from level routes on high fells and wild open moorland, ancient woodlands and forestry plantations, delightful riverside rambles and bracing coastal paths. There are scarcely any obstacles on any of theses tried and tested pushchair-friendly routes with accurate gradings and at-a-glance symbols to help select suitable walks.
£7.99

ALL-TERRAIN PUSHCHAIR WALKS: WEST YORKSHIRE
Rebecca Chippindale & Rebecca Terry
Pushchair-friendly routes in the spectacular countryside around the major towns of Keighley, Bradford, Leeds, Halifax, Huddersfield and Wakefield. There's woodland, moorland, canals, parks – and even some walks with a train journey in the middle – visiting a wide variety of locations including Ilkley Moor, Hardcastle Crags, Hebden Bridge and the River Wharfe.
£7.95

ALL-TERRAIN PUSHCHAIR WALKS: CHESHIRE

Norman Buckley

Enjoy these easy walks that range from the stunning peaks of East Cheshire to Mid-Cheshire's sandstone ridge, with the Cheshire plain in between. Amble along picturesque canal tow paths and disused railway lines or choose more adventurous walks through Macclesfield Forest. And as if that's not enough, there are visits to Cheshire's pretty villages, historic parklands and stately homes.

£7.95

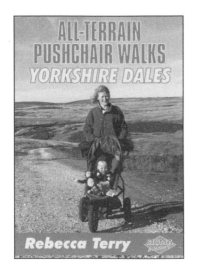

ALL-TERRAIN PUSHCHAIR WALKS: YORKSHIRE DALES

Rebecca Terry

Find out the best of what the Yorkshire Dales has to offer with these 30 tried and tested all-terrain pushchair walks through open moorland and country estates, and alongside the beautiful and dramatic rivers for which this National Park is renowned. The walks are all accurately graded and have at-a-glance symbols making choosing easier.

£7.95

Also available from Sigma

LAKELAND EASIEST WALKS
Suitable for wheelchairs, pushchairs and people with limited mobility
Doug & Margaret Ratcliffe

The Lake District and surrounding area has become far more accessible for wheelchairs and pushchairs in recent years. Although essentially a book for wheelchair users, these 38 specially selected short walks are all equally suitable for people with limited mobility and for very young children. Many of entries also have a 'points of interest' section describing features that can be seen from the paths and the photographs included illustrate the fact that a wheelchair or pushchair is no barrier to the wonderful Lakeland scenery.
£7.99

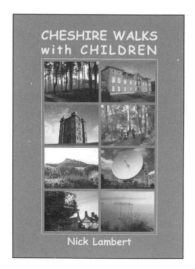

CHESHIRE WALKS WITH CHILDREN
2nd Edition
Nick Lambert
Now completely revised and updated, this was the first in our "walks with children" series and has quickly become a firm favourite. There are 30 walks, ranging in length, together with things to look out for and questions to answer along the way make it an entertaining book for young and old alike.
£8.99

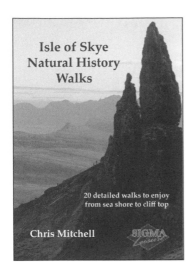

ISLE OF SKYE NATURAL HISTORY WALKS
20 detailed walks to enjoy from sea shore to cliff top
Chris Mitchell

An alternative guide to the wildlife and geology of Skye detailing where to see the island's lesser-known natural history. There are 20 walks based around Portree, Dunvegan, Broadford and Sleat together with detailed maps and quality photographs. Skye has long been regarded as a special place for the birdwatcher, the geologist, the botanist and marine biologist. By taking time to 'stand and stare' you will discover for yourself this hidden side of Skye – one that complements the traditional image of seascapes and mountain views. 70 colour photographs.
£9.99

THE CHARLIE CHAPLIN WALK
Stephen P Smith
This book is targeted at fans of Chaplin, those interested in film history, people with a connection to the Lambeth and Kennington areas of London and anybody with an interest of the social history of London's poor of the late Victorian and early Edwardian era. Explore the London streets of Charlie Chaplin's childhood in a chronological tour that can be taken on foot or from the comfort of an armchair. This book concentrates on the story of Chaplin's formative years and takes a fresh look at the influence they had upon his films.
£9.99

PEMBROKESHIRE WALKING
on the level
Norman and June Buckley

This is the sixth volume of the popular and well-established series of 'level walks' books. Discover both the breath-taking splendour of the Pembrokeshire coast and its diverse inland landscape. The 25 comparatively short, easy walks in this book include clear route directions, map and a brief description of features encountered along the way as well as recommendations for refreshment.
£8.99

NORTH WALES WALKING
on the level
Norman and June Buckley

This is the seventh volume of the popular and well-established series of 'level walks' books. There are 30 walks covering an area from The Great Orme to Cemlyn Bay. Whilst walks in North Wales are treasured by those who love the mountains, the balance of the book is much enhanced by the inclusion of the Conwy Valley and the Lleyn Peninsula, both part of the wider definition of Snowdonia, and by Anglesey, its near neighbour.
£8.99

All of our books are available through booksellers.
For a free catalogue, please contact:

**Sigma Leisure, Stobart House, Pontyclerc
Penybanc Road, Ammanford SA18 3HP**

Tel: 01269 593100 Fax: 01269 596116

info@sigmapress.co.uk   www.sigmapress.co.uk